James Rendel Harris

The Rest of the words of Baruch, a Christian Apocalypse of the year 136 A.D.

James Rendel Harris

The Rest of the words of Baruch, a Christian Apocalypse of the year 136 A.D.

ISBN/EAN: 9783337261566

Printed in Europe, USA, Canada, Australia, Japan

Cover: Foto ©Lupo / pixelio.de

More available books at **www.hansebooks.com**

THE REST OF THE WORDS

OF BARUCH.

London: C. J. CLAY AND SONS,
CAMBRIDGE UNIVERSITY PRESS WAREHOUSE.
AVE MARIA LANE.

Cambridge: DEIGHTON, BELL, AND CO.
Leipzig: F. A. BROCKHAUS.

THE REST OF THE WORDS
OF BARUCH:

A CHRISTIAN APOCALYPSE OF
THE YEAR 136 A.D.

THE TEXT REVISED WITH AN INTRODUCTION

BY

J. RENDEL HARRIS

FORMERLY FELLOW OF CLARE COLLEGE, CAMBRIDGE,
AND NOW PROFESSOR OF BIBLICAL LANGUAGES IN HAVERFORD COLLEGE,
PENNSYLVANIA.

LONDON:
C. J. CLAY AND SONS,
CAMBRIDGE UNIVERSITY PRESS WAREHOUSE.
1889

THE REST OF THE WORDS OF BARUCH.

THE present work is designed to draw attention to an important but hitherto much-neglected fragment of Apocalyptic literature which seems to me to be valuable, in spite of the contemptuous treatment which it has met with at the hands of the critics, both to the Ecclesiastical Historian and to the Christian Dogmatist; to the former, on account of the light which it throws on one of the most obscure periods in the growth of the Church, that, viz., which includes the revolt of the false Messiah; to the latter, because it helps us to see the manner in which one of the leading doctrines of the Christian Faith polarized the worshippers for and against itself (as almost every point of Christian doctrine does at some time or other in the history of the Church), and setting a man at variance spiritually with his fellow brought it to pass that the sword came down in the house itself to separate the undecided and half-hearted from the convinced and the faithful, that the many who were called might make way for the few who were chosen. And certainly when we say that in this tract the reader will hear the final farewell of the Church to the Synagogue, and that the parting words will be concerned with the doctrine of the Divine Nature of Jesus Christ, we have a right to ask for it a closer and a more careful perusal than it has hitherto met with. Nor is this the only reason why it should be made an object of attentive study. We hear much said now-a-days about the interpolation of Jewish Apocalypses by Christians, and it becomes a very interesting matter for critical study to determine how far such a tendency to the absorption and republication of earlier literary productions prevailed in those centuries which were especially marked by Apocalyptic activity, and in what manner that republication was commonly effected: for it is certain that in the early Christian literature we constantly disinter fragments

of earlier workmanship, and equally certain that nothing leads to
such reckless criticism as the unskilled or half-skilled attempt to
detach the embedded earlier form from its surroundings. The
present tract is one in which we are able to point out not only, as
I have intimated above, the exact date of its publication, but a
great part of the earlier material which the writer appropriated.
We can watch the bookmaker at his task, and can, so to speak,
mark the places where the scissors and paste have been used;
for this Apocalypse is the degenerate offspring of an illustrious
line, perhaps the very last scion of a noble house. The Apocalyptic
literature connected with Jeremiah and his companions must have
been extensive and popular, widely read and full of household
words; and a great part of this literature is still extant. We
are therefore favourably placed for the study of an interesting
problem in early religious teaching.

We may remark further that the Semitic and quasi-Semitic
literature is at its best in the region of Apocalypse: the historical
situations are better preserved because of the way in which
they have been disguised; the cipher in which the story was written has prevented the text from being tampered with. Apocalyptic writers do not deal in the flatteries which so often deface
ancient history. Josephus, for example, writing of the expected
Messiah and in the hope of pleasing his patrons, will have
Vespasian for his Coming One; but this adroit deviation from
popular belief would not be worth publication unless it were
made known both to the princes whom he designed to propitiate,
and to the masses whom he proposed to enlighten. If he had
held a contrary opinion or wished to inculcate it (for no one
knows what the real opinions of this agreeable diplomatist were)
he would have been obliged to write in allegory, cipher, or
Apocalypse, and for the few rather than the many. Vespasian
would have been an eagle or a dragon, or a dense forest or something of the kind. But we should at least be sure that we had
got at his real opinions. Apocalypses, then, are the truer by their
very falsity. The opinions which the writer disguises are his
genuine opinions.

Further than this, they are his opinions, generally speaking,
upon burning questions. Apocalypses concern themselves with
the most critical situations in the experiences of men and nations; they touch the deeper exigencies of life; they debate

the inconsistencies of man's conceptions of God and the Universe; they discourse on the Providence and Fore-ordination of the Almighty, as it were, to His very face. St Paul is content to state his belief that Adam sinned and, ergo, all men sinned. With the Apocalyptic Baruch or Ezra, the calm theological statement becomes a burning passionate question, "O thou Adam! wherefore hast thou sinned?" In the same way the decline of the Jewish polity is predicted or recorded with much calmness by the Apostles; "the wrath is come upon them to the uttermost" is the sum total of it; an Apocalyptist, on the contrary, is spurred to write not so much by the fact, as by grief over the fact. His head must needs be waters, and his eyes a fountain of tears. The highest national hopes, too, find their expression in this way: the coming of Messiah, the fall of Rome, the end of a captivity, the imminence of judgments,—all these things require bated breath in the speaker; and we hear him more clearly because he whispers. We know more of the national aspirations of the Jews from their Apocalypses than from all the histories that are extant: which is the same as saying that Apocalypse is one of the highest forms of historical record.

Our document furnishes us, as we shall see, with an illustration of the truth that almost all apocalyptic literature belongs to special historical crises: there are very few books of this kind which do not shew, in addition to disguised facts, disguised figures; the chronology is in cipher as well as the story: the number of years to Messiah's kingdom and to the fall of the great Eagle must be given, but not so that the great Eagle can read it. Time, times and half-a-time, says the Apocalyptist in answer to the passionate 'How long, Lord' which is being repeated inwardly by the people; and then a convenient key is given, and some note which shall epigrammatically attract attention, such as ὁ ἀναγινώσκων νοείτω, or a rude hexameter scrap, like

$$\text{Ὧδε ὁ νοῦς ὁ ἔχων σοφίαν.}$$

These crises in history and their associated revolutions in thought furnish the Apocalyptic situation: and it is therefore no surprise to us to find a redundance of this kind of literature near the period calculated for the birth of the Messiah, or subsequent to the fall of the city under Titus, or its further desolation under Hadrian. But there is one further point which is not so evident and which does not indeed lie in the nature of the case, but which is very important for the appreciation of Jewish Apocalypses; namely, the tendency which they shew to periodicity. The apocalyptic is not merely a prophet; he has become so by taking a cyclical view of the history of his people: that which furnishes his time-key in determining the duration of a captivity is the duration of a previous captivity. So many flights of the Phœnix, so many Jubilee periods, and then human things will return upon themselves. He expects God to repeat himself in history, and the more so as he sees history repeating itself. It was inevitable that the Jews should indulge Messianic hopes seventy years after the capture of the city by Titus: and they indulged them the more actively as the seventy years ran out.

Nor were they without some encouragement to this belief from actual event. One of the things written across Jewish history was the fatality connected with the 10th of Ab. We may get some idea of the import of this day by recalling the language of Josephus concerning it: "the fated round of times was come, the tenth day of the month Lous, on which aforetime the city had been burnt by the Babylonians" (*Bell. Jud.* VI. 4. 5). He does not hesitate to say that the time had been calculated by God; "one might rightly marvel at the accuracy of the cycle; for it was the very same month and day on which the city was formerly burnt by the Babylonians" (*Bell. Jud.* VI. 4. 8).

So deeply was this day marked with black in their calendar that there is reason to suspect that from that day to this it has been kept as a day of mourning both by Jews and Christians. With the Jews, of course, this is obvious: but the following considerations suggest that the Christian Church also shared this mourning with them. The Greek Church keeps a special memorial of the fall of the city on the 4th of November, and reads on that day, as we shall see, a portion of the very Apocalypse which we are engaged upon. But the question naturally arises as to how a memorial designed for the Fall of the City came to be read on this date. The answer is that Ab, which is the eleventh month of the Hebrew Calendar, has been replaced by November, the eleventh in the Julian year, while some reason not known to us has displaced the day from the tenth to the fourth[1]. We may,

---

[1] We shall see by and bye that our Christian Baruch has the month of Ab in his mind as the commencement of the Exile. According to the Talmud Bether was captured on the 9th of Ab.

therefore, suspect that Christians as well as Jews concerned themselves to note the fatal day[1]. And it was inevitable that the observed periodicity in the dated fortunes of the city should lead to a belief that the period of oppression would also run parallel with the history of the earlier Captivity. At all events this is a sufficient explanation of the excited state of the Jews in the last decade of the seventy years which followed the destruction of the city. Perhaps a similar consideration of other periods mentioned in history or prophecy will furnish us the explanation of the appearance of the other Apocalyptists, Ezras, or Jeremiahs, or Baruchs. This reasoning finds its confirmation when we proceed to the examination of our own especial document. We shall shew presently that it is a disguised history of the 66th year after the fall of the city: and the meaning attached to the number 66 is sufficiently evident from the fact that in many MSS. it has been corrected to 70. The number was seen to belong to the close of a cycle, what we may call the iron number of the captivity of Zion[2]. We will return to this point presently; but before discussing our Christian Baruch more closely, it is as well to say a few words about the earlier Apocalypses from which it is descended.

The Baruch literature begins, of course, with the Apocryphal Baruch of the Old Testament, a work which is still much in dispute, both as to the language in which it was written and the place and period to which it should be assigned. That it is præ-Christian may, however, probably be assumed; so that it differs from the rest of the writings which bear the name of Baruch, all of which belong to the period of the second Captivity (using this term for the result of the Roman War under Vespasian and Titus). At the same time this Apocryphal Baruch, though belonging to an earlier period, furnishes the suggestion for the later writings, and it may be anticipated before comparison that there will be numerous parallelisms in thought and expression between the

---

[1] We observe that the Menaeum heads the service for this day, Διήγησις εἰς τὸν θρῆνον τοῦ προφήτου Ἱερεμίου περὶ τῆς Ἱερουσαλήμ, καὶ εἰς τὴν ἅλωσιν ταύτης καὶ περὶ τῆς ἐκστάσεως Ἀβιμέλεχ. This of itself is strongly suggestive of the commemoration of the fatal day, and the allusion to the lamentation of Jeremiah shews that our tract has replaced an earlier book which was used in the commemoration service.

[2] The chronological parallels have been strained by the Jews to the detriment of the history, so as to make the Hadrian war last three years and a half; the time of the earlier hostilities: Renan rightly remarks (*Origines*, Vol. VI. p. 208, note) "ce dernier chiffre suspect; on a modelé le siége de Béther sur celui de Jérusalem."

early apocryphon, the prototype, and the later brood. But these parallelisms hardly come into account in what we are occupied about, and it is sufficient to refer to any of the good writers upon Apocalyptic literature for the verification of the relations that have been intimated. We call this book, for distinction, the Apocryphal Baruch (or simply Baruch).

With the next book, which we call the Apocalyptic Baruch, we have more to do; for not only is it a very important work, but, as we shall see, the connexion between it and our Christian Baruch is very marked. It was first published by Ceriani in *Monumenta Sacra et Profana*, Tom. I. fasc. i., from a Syriac MS. in the Ambrosian Library[1]; Ceriani at first reserved the Syriac for a future edition of the Old Testament, and gave only a Latin translation; but in response to appeals which were made to him by various scholars, he printed the whole of the Syriac text in the fifth volume of the *Monumenta*. Until Ceriani's publication nothing was known of this apocalyptic Baruch, except the letter of Baruch at the close of the book, which is extant in many MSS. and has often been printed. An examination of this book, in detail, is not within our scope; it will be sufficient to enumerate a few of the more definite results which come to light when the processes of criticism are applied to the book. First of all, then, the writer was a Jew, and a pious Jew, living in troublous times. He laments many who have deserted the Covenant and have cast from them the yoke of the Law, but consoles himself on the other hand that there are many 'who have left their vanities and taken refuge under the shadow of thy wings.' The last expression is the proper one for indicating proselytism. For example, it is the term used by the Jewish Fathers in describing the persuasive powers of the good Hillel; "the gentleness of Hillel brought us near under the wings of the Shekinah;" nor should we be wrong in inferring that those who have deserted the law have done so under the influence of an adverse proselytism which is undermining or replacing Judaism. The Law, too, is his last Jewish citadel. The city was in ruins when he wrote (and we need scarcely say that this desolation was not that of the Babylonian Captivity), and in the face of this disaster, the only religious anchorage was the Law; we know well the zeal with which the Jew turned in his exile from the

---

[1] The MS. is said to be as old as the sixth cent. Its class mark is B. 21 Inf. Ceriani has given a lithographic specimen of it.

Holy City to the pages of his holy book : "Unless thy law," said
Zion, "had been my delight, I should then have perished in my
affliction." To hold fast by the Law is the main precept ; and the
more so, because the end must be near: we pass away, but the
Law remains. The end of all things is at hand ; the pitcher is
near the fountain, the ship almost in the harbour, the journey has
the city in sight, life speeds to its ending: preaching and peni-
tence, alms and intercession have had their allotted season. Such
is the final sentiment of the apocalyptic writer, after he has given
his views of the Messianic Kingdom, of the fall of Rome, of the
future world and other matters which press upon the mind of the
God-fearing people.

And it is not difficult to see the period to which this lamentation belongs. He is a pious Jew of the time of the desertion of
Zion ; how long after the year A.D. 70 he lived and wrote is more
difficult to decide, and indeed no one has handled this point with
adequate clearness. We will indicate presently the chief opinions
which have been held.

Not only is the writer a Jew, but he is a Palestine Jew,—a
Jerusalem Jew, we may say with a good degree of confidence.
He is acquainted with the Holy City and its surroundings. The
imagined Baruch, for example, receives a word from the Lord
(c. 21) 'to go and sit in the valley of the Kedron in a cave of the
earth ;' how did he know that the Kedron valley was full of caves ?
In c. 47 he says, "Lo ! I am going to Hebron, for thither hath the
strong Lord sent me ;" he does not say, "I am going from Jerusalem to Hebron;" the city is taken for granted in the story. Add
to this, that Hebron would hardly be known out of Palestine.
The writer is a Jew, dwelling in the neighbourhood at least of the
Holy City ; we do not know how far the actual right of dwelling
in the city or its environs was restricted at this time ; it cannot
have been completely forbidden, for that is a regulation which
history shews and our later Baruch confirms to have been the result
of the revolt of Bar-Cochba. We shall shew presently that the
Christian Baruch was also written in the city or near it.

Returning to the question of the time when the Apocalyptic
Baruch was written, we observe that those who have written on
the subject have dealt with (1) its similarity to another, even
more famous Apocalypse, the fourth book of Ezra; (2) the evi-
dences of the influences of Christian Scriptures upon the writer;

(3) the actual notes of time which it contains; (4) the fact that it is quoted in the second century by Papias. For example: the connexion between fourth Ezra and the Apocalypse of Baruch, both in ideas and language, is undoubted.   P. Hofstede de Groot in his work on Basilides[1] determines the date of the fourth book of Ezra to be A.D. 97 (reign of Nerva), and he decides, in agreement with Volkmar, that at this time the Gospel of John was either unwritten, or current only in a limited circle. Then in a note he remarks that shortly before 4th Ezra there appeared the Apocalypse of Baruch, a work originally written in Greek, but transmitted to us only in Syriac, which is later than the destruction of the temple, earlier than Papias, and has references to Matthew, Luke and Romans. And this Apocalypse he affirms to be the work of a Jew. De Groot's conclusions may be traversed, perhaps, on some points, and we are not concerned to defend them; the connexion, however, between Ps. Ezra and Apocal. Baruch which he remarks is recognized by other writers; and the only question is whether Apocal. Baruch or Ps. Ezra is the earlier.

Fritzsche on the other hand, in his account of the Apocryphal Books of the Old Testament (Lips. 1871), will have it that the Apocalypse is written not long after the fall of the city. This is a good deal earlier than De Groot's estimate. H. Ewald[2] argues the date something as follows in his review of the earlier numbers of Ceriani's *Monumenta*. He points out that in c. 28 the reckoning from the destruction of the city to the expected Messiah is 'two parts weeks of seven weeks,' which he interprets to mean, in accordance with Hebrew parlance, two-thirds of 49 years: thus bringing us to the year 103 ($70 + \frac{2}{3}49$). But then allowing for twelve periods of final tribulation through which the world must pass from the time when the book is written until the end of the age, he subtracts 12 years and so brings us back to the year 91. It will be evident that this process of calculation and sub-calculation is very uncertain; and the same thing must be said of Ewald's other chronological points.

It is interesting to find, by way of contrast, that Hilgenfeld puts the date as far back as A.D. 72[3]!

---

[1] *Basilides am Ausgange des Apostolischen Zeitalters*, Leipzig, 1868.

[2] *Gottingische gelehrte Anzeigen*, 1867, p. 1705 sqq.

[3] *Messias Judaeorum*, p. lxiii.

It is a difficult thing then to determine the date with precision; and it does not seem that the critics have arrived at any more definite conclusion as to the upper time-limit of the book, than that it was written after the Roman Captivity. For the lower limit the only evidence (apart from that afforded by our Christian Baruch) seems to be that there is good reason to believe that it was from the Apocal. Baruch that Papias derived his Chiliastic story about the rate of produce of corn and wine in the millennium. The passage of Papias is well known by frequent quotation: that of Baruch is sufficiently like to it (x. 29). "In one vine there shall be a thousand shoots, and one shoot shall produce a thousand clusters, and one cluster a thousand berries, and one berry shall give a cor of wine......And they shall eat (of the manna) who come to the end of that time." It must be admitted, however, that there are elements in Papias' story which do not seem to be reproduced here; so that even at the lower time-limit we are a little uncertain. Nor do we arrive at much greater certainty when we try to determine the date of the Apocal. Baruch by the companion volume, the 4th of Ezra. Ewald goes so far as almost to assume that the two books are twin sisters, and if either is earlier than the other it is Apocal. Baruch. But this again is very uncertain. What we do seem to have arrived at is that it is generally admitted that 4th Ezra and Apocal. Baruch are closely related; that Baruch shews some parallels with the Christian Gospels; that its time of production is in the last thirty years of the first century, and that there is some reason to believe it is quoted by Papias. It is unfortunate that we cannot speak with greater confidence, because, since the Christian Baruch as we shall see is exactly dated, we should have been able to get an estimate of the time between the publication of a Jewish Apocalypse and its appropriation by a Christian writer, which estimate might have served us as a rough guide in other and similar cases.

In addition to the three Baruch books to which we have been alluding (Apocryphal Baruch, or simply Baruch, Apocalyptic Baruch, and Christian Baruch) it is very likely that there are other Baruch and Jeremiah books which have perished. The titles Baruch and Jeremiah are interchangeable: our Christian book sometimes bears the name which we have adopted, *Rest of the words of Baruch*, and sometimes it is called the *Paralipomena of Jeremiah*. And it is probable that similar confusion has prevailed with regard to the Baruchs and Jeremiahs which are not now extant, but of which we find traces.

For example, we find that it is to an apocryphal Jeremiah that Euthalius refers the quotation in Ephes. v. 14, "Awake thou that sleepest &c." Others, I believe, suppose it to be taken from an Apocryphal Adam. There is much confusion in these references to Apocryphal authors: but we may well imagine that the sentences come from some unrecovered part of the Baruch-Jeremiah literature, earlier of course than the Apocalypse.

An apocryphal Baruch is alluded to in Hippolytus[1], as being the text-book of a Gnostic named Justin. This Baruch is one of the superior angels, and not a prophet. Hippolytus gives a sketch of the system of Justin, and describes the oath which the initiated take that they will not divulge the mysteries nor relapse from the Good One to the creature: after which the worshipper is introduced to the secrets of the order, and beholds " what eye hath not seen and ear hath not heard, and which have not entered into the heart of man." This is the passage which Euthalius regards St Paul in 1 Cor. ii. as quoting, not from Isaiah, but from Apocryphal Elias. As it is one of the chief Gnostic formulæ in Justin's system, it is at least conceivable that Elias may be a mistake for Baruch.

In the *Altercation of Simon the Jew and Theophilus the Christian*[2], a work of the fifth century, to which Harnack has recently drawn attention[3], there is an allusion to a book of Baruch, from which Theophilus quotes what he considers to be a convincing argument against Simon: "Quomodo ergo prope finem libri sui de nativitate eius et de habitu vestis et de passione eius et de resurrectione eius prophetavit dicens: Hic unctus meus, electus meus, vulvae incontaminatae iaculatus, natus et passus dicitur"? This is in answer to Simon's statement that "Baruch de Christo nihil meminit." The passage is not in any of our known books of Baruch.

In Cyprian's *Testimonia* iii. 29 there has been inserted in some MSS. a quotation from Baruch which has never been identified, as far as I know, in the known Baruch literature. It runs as follows: " Veniet enim tempus et quaeretis me vos et qui post

---

[1] *Philosophumena*, v. 24—27.

[2] *Texte und Untersuchungen*, Bd. I. Heft 3, Leipzig, 1883.

[3] See Schürer, *Neutest. Zeitgeschichte*, III. 83 (Eng. translation). Schürer's notes on the Baruch literature are very valuable.

vos cupiant audire verbum sapientiae et intellectus et non invenient. Nationes autem cupient videre sapientem et non continget eis; non quia decrit aut deficiet sapientia huius saeculi terrae sed neque decrit sermo legis saeculo. Erit enim sapientia in paucis vigilantibus et taciturnis et quietis sibi confabulantibus, quoniam quidam eos horrebunt et timebunt ut malos. Alii autem nec credent verbo legis Altissimi. Alii autem ore stupentes non credent, et credent et contradicentes erunt contrarii et impedientes spiritum veritatis. Alii autem erunt sapientes ad spiritum erroris, et pronuntiantes sicut Altissimi et Fortis dicta. Alii autem personales fidei : alii capaces et fortes in fide Altissimi et odibiles alieno." The passage is certainly in the Baruch manner, as we may see by comparing Apocal. Bar. c. 48, "Non enim multi sapientes reperientur illo tempore, et intelligentes singulares aliqui erunt : sed etiam qui sciunt, maxime conticescent......et dicent multi multis illo tempore: Ubinam occultavit se multitudo intelligentiae?" But we can hardly identify it with any known passage : so we must still leave a margin for lost literature under the names of Baruch and Jeremiah.

We come now to our special subject, the Christian Baruch, a work which, as we said at the commencement, has met with a somewhat cold reception from the learned. Fritzsche describes it as much later in date and inferior in character to the Apocalypse of Baruch[1]. De Groot speaks of it as belonging to the Gnostic school, whatever that may mean. Kneucker[2] calls it "a tasteless working over" of the Apocalypse of Baruch. Dillmann refers it to the third or fourth century, which can hardly be meant as a commendation. Schürer is more guarded, and simply says that it is "a Christian book akin to our Apocalypse of Baruch, and has borrowed largely from it." The question of the literary excellence of the work is of course quite a subordinate one; it is of more importance to know that it is admittedly and obviously a Christian book ; and therefore not to be despised even if it should turn out to be of the third or fourth century. But the fact is, as we have said, it is much earlier, and its chronology is susceptible of exact determination.

---

[1] He expressed a hope of editing it, however, at some future time; a promise which he does not seem to have redeemed; 18 years having elapsed since the announcement.

[2] *Das Buch Baruch*, Lips. 1879, p. 195.

We will first of all shew that the book was written by a Judæo-Christian living in the city of Jerusalem. The action of the story, being concerned with the exile of the people, is divided between Jerusalem and Babylon; but the writer betrays himself by an excessive knowledge of the topography of the Holy City. Jeremiah wishes to send Abimelech the Ethiopian away from the city in order that he may not see the destruction thereof: and the Lord directs him to send him *to the gardens of Agrippa*, where he shall be hidden in the mountain side until the return of the people from exile. Accordingly Jeremiah directs Abimelech to take a basket and go to the garden of Agrippa *by the mountain road* and bring back figs. Abimelech goes, falls asleep under a tree, wakes after a sufficient sleep of 66 years, and coming back to the ruined city fails to recognize it. "Alas!" says he, "I have lost my way because I took the mountain road."

Now the mention of the garden of Agrippa would of itself be a sufficient betrayal of the locality of the writer, but when it is intimated that there were two roads thither, we are not only convinced that the writer was speaking of a spot well-known to him, but we are even encouraged to attempt an identification of the spot mentioned. It is very likely that the gardens of Herod alluded to are in the fertile valley below Solomon's pools, frequently spoken of by travellers and their guides as Solomon's gardens, and bearing to-day the name of Artas, which is an evident perversion of the Roman *hortus*. I know no more likely place for a royal garden in the vicinity of Jerusalem. And the curious thing is that there are decidedly two roads from Jerusalem to Artas; one the high-road to Bethlehem and Hebron, with a short divergence to the left at Solomon's pools; and the other the track round the hills which follows the line of Solomon's aqueduct from the pools to the city. It certainly looks as if the geography were real geography; and if this be the case the book was written in Jerusalem, as was its prototype the Apocalypse of Baruch. And in any case the allusion to the gardens of Agrippa remains whether we have correctly identified their position or not.

But we may go further than this: not only have we a geographical limit in the gardens of Agrippa, but we have also both superior and inferior chronological limits. Superior, by the fact that the book was written later than Agrippa whichever of the family may be intended; inferior, because it could not be written after the time when his name ceased to be popularly attached to the place described. And it seems to me that this consideration alone would be fatal to Dillmann's hypothesis of the third or fourth century as the time of production of the book. The writer then is a Jerusalem Christian.

The next thing is to give the chronological identification. We have already alluded to this by anticipation. The word of the Lord to Jeremiah concerning Abimelech is that "I will cover him in the mountain *until I cause the people to return to the city.*" Now on the hypothesis, allegorical and cyclical, of a Babylonian captivity, the conventional duration of exile is 70 years. Yet the writer makes Abimelech fall asleep for 66 years. The Greek service-book corrects this to 70, and inserts the 70 again in the passage where Abimelech, meeting the old man outside of the city, obtains from him the information that Jeremiah is with the people in Babylon; where it adds the words 'since 70 years.' The correction was perfectly natural and every way likely: but we must read sixty-six years, and not seventy. The same exchange of numbers will be found in c. vi. where Abimelech shews his basket of figs, and remarks that, though sixty-six years had elapsed since they were gathered, they were not spoiled. And since this is the date of the suggested return from exile, and the book professes to be describing contemporary movements (for it records almost nothing of subsequent date), then the year of the expected return is A.D. 70 (the date of the Captivity) + 66 years = A.D. 136, and the book must have been written very soon after that time.

Very soon after; because, as we shall see, it is an Eirenicon addressed to the people of that time, a time marked perhaps more deeply than any other in the history both of Jews and Christians (unless perhaps it be the capture of the city by Titus), when severe political regulations produced greater changes in six months in the relations of the Church and Synagogue than had taken place in all the preceding years of the century. We know very little, as we would wish to know, of the details of the new settlement of Jewish affairs by Hadrian: but we learn from the history and the coins that Jerusalem was no more, that it was replaced by Aelia Capitolina; that the plough was passed over the sacred soil in token of its renewed subjugation; that Roman statues, the emperor and his gods, were in the holy places; and that an edict

of the emperor prohibited the Jew from approaching the holy
city. Turning to the lists of bishops in Eusebius, we find that
Gentile names appear now for the first time. It is not necessary
to assume the accuracy of Eusebius' list of Jerusalem bishops;
many of these lists, especially the earlier portions of them, are
afterthoughts. But the tradition which makes Marcus bishop of
Jerusalem at the close of the Hadrian War can hardly be in-
correct. It means at least that there has been, from political
necessity, a change in the organic life of the Church. The last
have become first, and the first last. The Judæo-Christian party
with its antique traditions and venerable Mosaism is passing away.
The breach with Judaism, which Paul usually effected in a few
months in any city where he laboured, was not really accomplished
in Jerusalem until the false Messiah had run his course. But
then when it came, it came quickly.

Now our document is the Church's Eirenicon to the Synagogue,
at the time of the Hadrian edict. The problem is, how to evade
the edict of banishment from the holy City which is pronounced
on the race. Granted that we are carried away captive, and that
there is a possibility of return from captivity, how is this return
to be brought about ? And the answer is contained in the letter
which Baruch is instructed to send from Jerusalem to Jeremiah in
Babylon. So we find in c. vi. as follows: "If ye obey my voice,
saith the Lord, by the mouth of Jeremiah, I will separate you
from Babylon ; but he that will not obey, let him be as *a stranger
to Jerusalem* (ξένος τῆς Ἱερουσαλήμ), and I will test you by the
water of Jordan, and there he that will not obey will be made
manifest." If nothing more had been said, we should have con-
jectured that this meant the rite of baptism ; but lest we should
have any doubt on the matter, the writer continues parenthetically,
" this is the sign of the great seal," the conventional Patristic term
for baptism. It is possible that these words may be a later interpolation, but they are not the less striking on that account, for
they would disclose the interpretation that primitively attached
to the passage. The meaning of it all is that the Christians, who
are evidently not affected by the imperial edict, for they took no
part in the rebellion, have suggested to Jews that by becoming
Christians by the way of baptism they can evade the force of the
edict, and no longer be *strangers to Jerusalem*. The people are
to be brought down to Jordan's side from Babylon, and there the

precious and the vile are as far as possible to be separated one from another. Those that will make the necessary renunciation are received, the rest rejected. The story runs that Jeremiah sorted them out by families, and when a whole family was clear in renouncing Babylon and its customs they were accepted, and if not they were rejected. It is not easy to imagine the manner of the selection. The writer does not mean Rome when he speaks of the people renouncing Babylon and passing over Jordan, and talks of mixed families where men had married Babylonish women. I think he here means the old school of Jews (those who are Babylonians by choice and who make no move towards Jordan), between whom and the Gentile Church lies the conflict for the possession of the intermediate party, the Judæo-Christians of various types. The selection being made by families is thoroughly in the Eastern manner, where religion is always bounded by social and racial limits, just as population is to this day reckoned by households. "Himself believed and his house" is the conventional formula for a change of religion: "as for me and my house" is a similar term. What makes one a little more confident in this interpretation that it was an appeal on the part of the Gentile Christians or at least of the Gentilising Christians to the more conservative, half convinced among their Jewish brethren, is that we find from the account that some undecided people in the middle ground came part way to Jerusalem and then returned; and that on their returning to Babylon, they were received with an intimation that as they had secretly departed from them, they would not be received again: Babylon would have none of them. This according to the story leads to the formation of a new colony which is derisively called Samaria. Now this is not difficult of interpretation, if we imagine that there were those who had gone so far from Judaism as to provoke an edict against their being received again into ecclesiastical fellowship, and yet had not come so near to Christianity as to be able to pass the baptismal standards. In this case, then, one result of the Hadrian edict is the formation of a new Ebionite movement in Palestine. This exactly agrees with the statements of Epiphanius and Jerome as to the origin of Ebionism: they attempted to be both Jews and Christians, and ended by being neither.

It is just possible that this accepting and rejecting of families of Jews by unauthorized or half-authorized persons may be the origin of a story in the Talmud which seems to cover some irrita-tion of national feeling[1] on the subject of proselytism.

The story is apparently referred to the time of Rabbi Joshua who is talmudically the second generation from Hillel the Great.

"R. Joshua said, I received from R. Johanan ben Zakkai, who received it from his teacher as a tradition in a direct line from Moses on Mount Sinai, that Elias would not come to pronounce clean or unclean, *to reject or admit families* in general, but only to reject those that had entered by violence, and to admit those who had been rejected by violence. There was, beyond Jordan[2], a family of the name of Beth Zerefa, which a certain Ben Zion *had excluded by violence*. There was there another family (of impure blood) whom this Ben Zion had *admitted by violence*. He comes to pronounce such clean or unclean, to reject or to admit them." It is quite possible that this story refers to the admission of proselytes by Jewish Christians of the city of Jerusalem (note the Ben Zion) who rank practically in the city as Jews, at all events up to the time of the final rupture, although in foreign cities they had long been known as a 'third race.'

In Jerusalem itself the line of demarcation between Jews and Christians was for a long time very faintly marked. The ecclesia was *intra synagogam*. Witness the account of the relations between the Pharisees and S. James the Just which Hegesippus furnishes; no difference of opinion seems to exist, except on the one point of the person of Jesus Christ, whom St James affirms to be coming in the clouds of heaven. Something of the same sort is implied in the story of Stephen. We shall see by and bye that this is the very point which provokes the people in the story to stone Jeremiah, just as in the history they had done to St James.

We have shewn, then, that the date suggested by the Baruch-story is exactly the right date for the interpretation of the events that are there adumbrated. It is very interesting to see that baptism, which at first served to initiate proselytes into Judaism,

---

[1] Mishna *Edujoth*, viii. 7, quoted in Schürer *Neutest. Zeitgesch.* ii. 156, Eng. trans.

[2] We must not strain allegory in order to see here a reference to baptism. I use the passage to shew that the Jews in the first century quarrelled over and discussed their family membership and its purity or impurity just as our Apocalypse shews them to be doing in the early part of the second century.

but which does not seem to have been applied to Jews of good standing, has now become one of the means for distinguishing the Jews from the proselytes, and that the baptized are baptizing the baptizers.

Before leaving the question of chronology, we must say a word or two about another time-note in the book. The people stone Jeremiah, and when dying he predicts the coming of Jesus Christ, the Son of God, after a lapse of four hundred and seventy-seven years[1]. It is a little difficult to see what he means by these figures and how he arrives at them. It must be either that the Apocalyptist is giving the actual period from the first return from Exile to the Messiah, or he is fabricating a similar period for the second advent, the numbers being assumed to repeat as in the case of the duration of the Exile. That the former is the right interpretation may be gathered from the prediction which Jeremiah makes that the Messiah will choose to himself 12 apostles in order that they may preach the gospel amongst the Gentiles. (c. ix. 18.) But how does he calculate the period? For we have no possibility of deducing 477 years from the interval between Jeremiah's death and the birth of Christ. The building of the walls under Ezra and Nehemiah is, however, not very far from the time intimated; if we assume this to have taken place in 458 B.C. or thereabout we should not be 20 years out in the reckoning. But it would be idle to assume a great acquaintance with chronology on the part of our simple-minded Apocalyptist; and we might perhaps leave this part of the question unsettled without feeling that the interpretation would suffer. We will, however, venture one suggestion for clearing the matter up. At the close of the sixth book of Josephus' Jewish Wars will be found a table of the leading periods in the history of Jerusalem from conquest to conquest and captivity to captivity. Now in this list the time from David to the Babylonian exile is given as 477 years: so that it is just possible that the Apocalyptist made an error in taking a number from Josephus' tables.

We will now pass on to consider the literary debts of the Christian Baruch to his predecessors, beginning with some passages which are founded on the Apocalypse of Baruch.

Apocal. ii. Haec autem dixi tibi, ut dicas Jeremiae, et omnibus qui similes sunt vobis, ut recedatis ab urbe ista, quia opera vestra

[1] The mss. are very confused over this number; the Ethiopic in particular fluctuating between 303, 330, and 333 *weeks*.

sunt urbi huic tanquam columna firma et preces vestrae tanquam murus validus.

This passage is imitated in the later Baruch as follows: c. i. 1, ἔξελθε ἐκ τῆς πόλεως ταύτης σὺ καὶ ὁ Βαρούχ......αἱ γὰρ προσευχαὶ ὑμῶν ὡς στῦλος ἑδραῖός ἐστιν ἐν μέσῳ αὐτῆς καὶ ὡς τεῖχος ἀδαμάντινον περικυκλοῦν αὐτόν. (We are thus able to restore some parts of the original Greek of the Apocalypse of Baruch.)

The remote source of either sentence is to be sought in Jer. i. 18.

Apocal. vi. Et factum est crastino die, et ecce exercitus Chaldaeorum circumdedit urbem, et tempore vesperae reliqui populum ego Baruch et exivi et steti apud quercum : et contristabar super Sion et ingemiscebam super captivitatem quae supervenerat populo : et ecce subito spiritus fortitudinis sustulit me et extulit me supra Jerusalem in altum. et vidi et ecce quatuor angeli stantes super quatuor angulos urbis, tenentes unusquisque ex eis lampada ignis in manibus suis.

Compare with this the account by the later Baruch of the capture of the city, especially

iii. 2. Καὶ ἐγένετο φωνὴ σάλπιγγος, καὶ ἐξῆλθον ἄγγελοι ἐκ τοῦ οὐρανοῦ, κατέχοντες λαμπάδας ἐν ταῖς χερσὶν αὐτῶν, καὶ ἔστησαν ἐπὶ τὰ τείχη τῆς πόλεως.

The angels then in Bar. Apocal. wait until one of their number takes the holy vessels and delivers them to the earth, which opens her mouth and swallows them up. The Christian Baruch makes this hiding of the vessels to be done by Jeremiah and Baruch.

x. Dic Jeremiae ut vadat et confirmet captivitatem populi usque ad Babylonem ; tu autem mane hic in vastitate Sion et ego ostendam tibi post hos dies quod futurum est ut contingat in fine dierum. et dixi Jeremiae sicut praecepit mihi Dominus. et ipse quidem ivit cum populo ; ego autem Baruch reversus sum et sedi ante portas templi et lamentatus sum lamentationem istam super Sion et dixi.

The whole of these details are absorbed by the later Baruch, with the single exception of the mention of the 'gates of the temple.' Each writer makes Baruch the one that laments over the city.

A more striking case of absorption of the earlier story is the account of the priests throwing the keys of the Sanctuary up to heaven.

Apocal. x. Vos autem sacerdotes sumite claves sanctuarii et proiicite in altitudinem coeli et date eas Domino et dicite; Custodi domum tuam tu: nos enim ecce inventi sumus oeconomi mendaces.

Bar. Christ. iv. 3. Ἰερεμίας δὲ ἄρας τὰς κλεῖδας τοῦ ναοῦ, ἐξῆλθεν ἔξω τῆς πόλεως καὶ ἔρριψεν αὐτὰς ἐνώπιον τοῦ ἡλίου, λέγων· Σοὶ λέγω, ἥλιε, λάβε τὰς κλεῖδας τοῦ ναοῦ τοῦ Θεοῦ, καὶ φύλαξον αὐτὰς ἕως ἡμέρας ἐν ᾗ ἐξετάσει σε Κύριος περὶ αὐτῶν. Διότι ἡμεῖς οὐχ εὑρέθημεν ἄξιοι τοῦ φυλάξαι αὐτὰς, ὅτι ἐπίτροποι ψεύδους ἐγενήθημεν.

The passage in *Apocal.* xi. Dicite mortuis: Beati vos magis quam nosmetipsi, qui vivi sumus, becomes in *Bar. Christ.* iv. 9 Μακάριοί εἰσιν Ἀβραὰμ Ἰσαὰκ καὶ Ἰακὼβ, ὅτι ἐξῆλθον ἐκ τοῦ κόσμου τούτου.

It will be seen that the coincidences in the opening chapters of the two Apocalypses are very marked. The same coincidence is to be traced on referring to the closing chapters of the Apocalyptic Baruch. Baruch writes a letter to the nine and a half tribes who are in Babylon and sends it by means of an eagle.

Apocal. lxxvi. Accersivi aquilam et locutus sum ei verba ista: Te fecit Altissimus ut sis excelsior prae omnibus avibus: et nunc vade, neque commoreris in loco, neque ingrediaris nidum, neque consistas super quamvis arborem, donec transieris latitudinem aquarum multarum fluminis Euphratis, et ieris ad populum illum qui habitat ibi et proice ad eos epistolam hanc: recordare autem quod tempore diluvii a columba accepit Noe fructum olivae cum eam emisisset de arca; sed et corvi ministrarunt Eliae deferentes ei cibum, sicut praeceptum erat eis; etiam Salomon tempore regni sui quocumque volebat mittere, aut quaerere aliquid, avi praecipiebat, et obediebat ei sicut praecipiebat ei: et nunc ne taedeat te, neque declines ad dexteram aut ad sinistram, sed vola et vade via recta ut custodias mandatum Fortis sicut dixi tibi. (lxxvii.) Et fuit cum consummassem omnia verba epistolae huius et scripsissem eam cum cura usque ad finem eius et plicuissem eam et obsignassem eam diligenter et ligassem eam ad collum aquilae et dimisi et misi eam.

This is imitated in c. vii. of the Christian Baruch with no loss of force in the transcription:

Bar. Christ. vii. Σοὶ λέγω, βασιλεῦ τῶν πετεινῶν, ἄπελθε ἐν εἰρήνῃ μεθ' ὑγείας καὶ τὴν φάσιν ἔνεγκέ μοι. Μὴ ὁμοιωθῇς τῷ κόρακι ὃν ἐξαπέστειλε Νῶε, καὶ οὐκ ἀπεστράφη εἰς τὴν κιβωτόν·

ἀλλὰ ὁμοιώθητι τῇ περιστερᾷ ἥτις ἐκ τρίτου φάσιν ἤνεγκε τῷ
δικαίῳ· οὕτω καὶ σύ, ἆρον τὴν καλὴν φάσιν ταύτην τῷ Ἰερεμίᾳ,
καὶ τοῖς σὺν αὐτῷ, ἵνα εὖ σοι γένηται, ἆρον τὴν χάρτην ταύτην
τῷ λαῷ τῷ ἐκλεκτῷ τοῦ Θεοῦ. Ἐὰν κυκλώσωσί σε πάντα τὰ
πετεινὰ τοῦ οὐρανοῦ, καὶ πάντες οἱ ἐχθροὶ τῆς ἀληθείας βουλόμενοι πολεμῆσαι μετὰ σοῦ, ἀγώνισαι· ὁ Κύριος δώῃ σοι δύναμιν.
Καὶ μὴ ἐκκλίνῃς εἰς τὰ δεξιὰ ἢ ἀριστερά, ἀλλ᾽ ὡς βέλος ὕπαγον
ὀρθῶς οὕτως ἄπελθε κτέ.

These instances will be sufficient to shew the kind of use which
the later Apocalyptist made of the earlier. And that the earlier
form had attached to it the epistle of Baruch appears not only
from the legend of the carrier-eagle but from the admission[1] at
the close of the Christian Baruch that "the rest of the words of
Jeremiah and all his might are written, not here, but in the
epistle of Baruch."

The traces of the use of the beautiful Apocalypse, known as
the fourth book of Ezra, are less marked, but they are decided.
The famous passage in c. v. foretelling that "blood shall drop
from wood *and the stone shall utter its voice*" was known to our
Apocalyptist: it furnished him with the idea of the closing situation
in his book; that in which Jeremiah sets up a stone, which takes
his likeness, and deceives thereby the people who wish to kill him,
until he has finished communicating the mysteries which he has
seen to the crowd and his companions Baruch and Abimelech.
The riotous folk stone the stone, thinking it to be Jeremiah.
But at last the stone cries out with a human voice, "O foolish
children of Israel, wherefore do ye stone me, thinking that I am
Jeremiah?" The motive for this story is evidently the single
sentence quoted above from Ezra[2]. Another clause in the same
connexion, where Ezra foretells amongst the signs of the end
that "salt water shall be found in sweet water and friends be at
war with one another," is copied by the Christian writer (c. ix.
16), "Snow shall become black and sweet waters salt."

The writer was also acquainted with the Apocryphal Isaiah.
In c. ix. 18, 19 the text of our author runs as follows: "He shall
come, and he shall come forth and he shall choose him twelve

---

[1] This may however be a later appendix.

[2] IV. Esd. v. 5. It is quite possible that the whole sentence is a confused allusion to the sawing asunder of Isaiah and the stoning of Jeremiah, and that Ezra
himself may be drawing on legendary sources: but compare what is said on this
point on pp. 43, 44.

apostles that they may preach the Gospel amongst the Gentiles: whom I beheld adorned by his Father and coming into the world on the mount of Olives; and he shall fill the hungry souls. While Jeremiah was saying these things concerning the Son of God, that he is coming into the world, the people was enraged, and said; These are the same words as were spoken by Isaiah the son of Amos, when he said, I beheld God and the son of God. Come then and let us kill him with a different death to that wherewith we killed Isaiah." The people are not alluding here immediately to the famous sixth chapter of Isaiah in which the prophet sees the Lord on his throne, or as the Targumists prefer to render it, so as to avoid the anthropomorphic conception, the glory of the Lord on his throne[1]; but they are speaking of a prophecy or pseudo-prophecy in which the manner of his death seems also to have been recorded as well as his ecstasy. And this can hardly be anything else than the Ascension of Isaiah, in which Justin Martyr is supposed to have found his information about the sawing in twain of Isaiah with a wooden saw, and to which Origen definitely appealed as an authority for the manner of the prophet's martyrdom. We will not saw him asunder, they say, as Isaiah was martyred, but, for the sake of variety, we will stone him. It is, of course, possible that the writer might have based his fiction on mere traditions, but the reference to Jeremiah as seeing the coming of the Son of God and his sending forth of the twelve apostles to preach is conclusive in favour of the Ascension of Isaiah as the origin from which he drew. The reason why Isaiah is arrested is because " Berial was in great wrath against Isaiah on account of the vision and the revelation which Sammael had unveiled and because by him was seen the coming of the Beloved from the seventh heaven, and his transformation,...and the tortures wherewith the children of Israel would torture him, and the coming and the teaching of the twelve apostles..."[2] And that the writer had the actual book to refer to will appear from the use he has made of another detail of the Martyrdom of Isaiah. When the writer describes the tortures of the prophet and his final ascent in rapture through the seven heavens before his death, he makes the prophet fall into a death-like trance in which speech and breathing cease. And

[1] A conception which lies underneath the passage in the Gospel: "He saw his glory and spake of him," John xii. 41.
[2] *Ascensio Isaiae*, ed. Dillmann, c. iii.

what Isaiah sees in that vision he tells afterwards to the king and
the circle of the prophets. "While he was speaking by the Holy
Ghost, in the hearing of all, he held his peace and his mind was
rapt away and taken upward so that he saw not those that stood
around; his eyes were open but his mouth was still and the mind
of his body was rapt away upward, but his breath was in him, for
he saw a vision." (I think that we should read here 'his breath
was *not* in him.') The writer explains further that the "vision
which he saw was not of this world, but of the world which is
hidden from mortal eyes. And after Isaiah saw this vision, he
narrated it to Hezekiah and Josab his son and the rest of the
assembled prophets." All of this is imitated in our Christian
Baruch: Jeremiah falls into a death-like trance, but after three
days he revives, his soul revisits her tenement, and he tells the
Glory of the Father and the Son. This use of Apocryphal Isaiah
begins in the earlier part of the prophet's ecstasy (c. ix. 3) where
he cries out "Holy, holy, holy...beyond the sweet voice of the two
seraphim:" here the direct reference is to Isaiah vi., as is seen
from the trisagion and the mention of two seraphim ("one cried
unto another"), but that Ps. Isaiah is in mind with its full Chris-
tology appears from the insertion of the words "the true light that
lighteneth me."

We need not hesitate to say then that the writer has used the
Ascension of Isaiah, and used it too, for it is an interpolated Apocalypse, augmented and expanded by Christian hands, in its later
and Christian form. The date of this work is discussed by Dillmann in his preface, and we need not dispute his conclusion in
referring the book to the beginning of the second century[1].

We have thus determined three earlier Judæo-Christian works
which have been used and imitated in the process of manufacture
of the Christian Baruch. We will pass on to examine the possible
use which the writer may have made of other traditions concerning
Jeremiah, or, which is for our purpose the same thing, of lost books
incorporating traditions.

That traditions concerning Jeremiah were widely circulated in
early times appears from many considerations: the second book of
the Maccabees, for instance, has the whole story of the hiding of
the sacred vessels, in a form which does not agree with the Apo-

---

[1] *Ascensio*, p. xvi. Quibus omnibus perpensis Ascensionem iam primis secundi
sacculi decenniis exstitisse censeo.

calyptic Baruch, and which is not in perfect harmony with the Christian Baruch. And its version professes to be that of official documents. "It is also found in the records that Jeremiah the prophet commanded them that were carried away to take some of the fire, as it hath been signified: and that the prophet on giving them the law charged them that were carried away not to forget the commandments of the Lord, and that they should not be led astray in their minds on seeing images of silver and gold with their ornaments. And with other such admonitions exhorted he them that the law should not depart from their heart. It is also contained in the writing that the prophet being warned of God commanded that the tabernacle and the ark should be brought along after him: and that he went forth into the mountain where Moses climbed up and saw the heritage of God. And Jeremiah on coming thither found a kind of cave-dwelling, and he carried in there the tabernacle and the ark and the altar of incense and closed up the door. And certain of those that followed him came up to mark the way and they could not find it. But when Jeremiah learned of it, he blamed them and said, The place shall be unknown until God gather his people again together, and become propitious. And then shall the Lord shew these things[1]."

There is one point in which the later Baruch agrees better with this than the Apocalypse: it makes Jeremiah hide the vessels and not the angels. Possibly, therefore, the writer was under the influence of the Maccabean tradition, which need not be very early. The date of the second of Maccabees is, however, one of the unsolved problems.

Another very important tradition concerning Jeremiah is that he was stoned. This is not an original idea of the Christian Baruch. We find it in the Epistle to the Hebrews. The famous passage "they were stoned, they were sawn asunder, &c." is a summary of the sufferings of the worthies of Faith, and each statement is based on the history of some real person: it has always been known that "they were sawn asunder" referred to Isaiah, just as "stopped the mouths of lions" referred to Daniel, and "quenched the violence of fire" to the three Hebrew children; but it is not so generally felt that "they were stoned" belongs to Jeremiah.

[1] 2 Macc. ii.

Yet such is the case, as the Baruch-Jeremiah legends shew:
and the Epistle to the Hebrews is therefore one of the early wit-
nesses to the tradition. But whence was it derived? We may
not easily reply, but it was from the same source in written or
unwritten tradition that Christian Baruch derived his information.

There is other important evidence of the diffusion of the
tradition. The place of burial of Jeremiah is still shewn in Jerusalem in a cave which passes by the name of Jeremiah's grotto.
This grotto lies in the southern side of the conspicuous hill to the
north of the city which is supposed by many persons to be the
place called Calvary. On the north-west side of the same hill are
the ruins of the early Church which commemorated the martyrdom of St Stephen who was said to have been stoned here. And
it is said that this hill is the Tarpeian rock of ancient Jerusalem,
the Beth-hassaqelah or 'Place of Stoning' of the Talmud. It
seems then that there is some connexion between the death
which Jeremiah met, according to tradition, and the place where
he is said to be buried. And the tradition concerning his stoning
in Jerusalem must be early: for the uniform church tradition of
later days, as we find it in the life of Jeremiah attributed falsely
to Epiphanius, or the life that is given on his commemoration
day in the Greek Church (see Menaeum for May 1), is that he was
stoned indeed, but at Tahpanhes in Egypt, and not, as the Jerusalem tradition and the Christian Baruch say, in Jerusalem. Can
we be wrong in affirming the antiquity of the tradition which we
find in our authority? The opinion of the first and second centuries seems to be that Jeremiah was stoned in Jerusalem[1].

But did the traditions of our document centre round any
actual person? Are Jeremiah and Baruch the background of the
picture or the foreground? Do the historical features of the
romance limit themselves to the City and the time of the Jewish
expulsion and the baptismal suggestion of the Christians to the
Jews: or may we go further? The writer has, according to some

[1] I do not forget that an attempt might have been made to bring the legends
into harmony with our Lord's words "O Jerusalem which killest the prophets and
stonest them that are sent unto thee;" but such a tendency would not have
produced an earlier tradition but a later one. It is more reasonable, though the
hypothesis is not necessary, and might even be fanciful, to understand our Lord as
saying this in allusion to the legends. When he said it he was in view of the place
of supposed martyrdom of Isaiah on the south of the city and of Jeremiah on the
north.

MSS., changed 'Baruch the scribe' of the old Testament into 'Baruch the reader.' Does he mean a real official of the Church? It would be hard to say: but with Jeremiah the case is easier: for there is reason to believe that Judah, the last bishop of Jerusalem before the definitely Christian régime, died at the hands of the party of Bar-cochba. The Chronicon of Eusebius declares that many of the Christians suffered for not taking arms against Rome; and marks the close of the war by the arrival of the first Gentile Bishop. Now if Judah the supposed fifteenth bishop had outlived the war, he would certainly not have been exiled by the Romans: so he must have vacated his office by death.

A further interesting question arises with regard to the relations of our writer to the Christian records. We see him quoting freely and incorporating adroitly from many of the Judæo-Christian books which were current at that time in Palestine; Isaiah, Ezra, and Baruch—he knows them all. Baruch the Apocalyptist, whom he quotes most freely, though hardly to be called a Christian, has been affirmed by careful critics to be under the influence of the sentiments and to shew traces of the language of our Gospels. What of the Christian Baruch? Had he any acquaintance with the New Testament Scriptures? *There is some ground for believing that he was acquainted with the Gospel of John.* This will no doubt sound somewhat strange, but we will not prejudge the question by choosing for the time of production of the fourth gospel a period as *late* as is consistent with what has been hitherto known of the literature of the second century: there has been too much *à priori* reasoning in the dating of the fourth Gospel. Nor is the Nemesis which attaches to this arbitrary and *ex silentio* criticism exhausted. Neither will we on the other hand over-emphasise coincidences of thought and expression between our writer and the Gospel; although it might be possible to argue that when a writer (ix. 13) calls Jesus Christ the light of all the ages, the unquenchable lamp, the life of the faith, it is natural to refer to the Light of the World, the Light of Men and the Light of Life, and to the contrast which Christ makes between himself and John the Baptist, when he calls him the lamp *which has been kindled* and shines. We might point out also that the conjunction of φῶς and ζωή is frequently recognized as not merely Christian, but Johannine. M. Clermont-Ganneau has established a number of cases of the occurrence of φῶς + ζωή as a

Christian formula in Syria. The two words are often arranged crosswise, thus $\phi \overset{z}{\omega} c$; and M. Ganneau says we must seek the origin of the formula in the Gospel of John[1]. And with less judgment it would be possible to quote the words (ix. 18) ἐρχόμενον εἰς τὸν κόσμον as a reminiscence of John i. 9, the interpretation of which is however doubtful. As none of these coincidences would definitely convince me of a quotation from John, so neither do I unduly desire to convince any one by them; but I would draw attention to one clause in the adoration of Jeremiah (ix. 3) where he addresses the Lord as τὸ φῶς τὸ ἀληθινὸν τὸ φωτίζον με, the true Light that lighteneth me: where the collocation of words is so peculiar, that it is almost impossible to refer the language to any other than St John, and in view of this fact the previous coincidences acquire new force. Further the passage is found, not only in the Greek, which exhibits at many points a text that has undergone some correction, but in the Ethiopic version, which often approaches very nearly, as we shall see, to the original form of the Apocalypse. Unless then it can be shewn that these words are a later addition, in the Ethiopic as well as in the Greek, we must admit a quotation from the fourth Gospel, which quotation happily allows of being dated in or about the year 136 A.D.

Authorities for the Text.

In the year 1866 Dillmann published the Ethiopic version of the Christian Baruch from several MSS.; and in the preface to the Ethiopic Chrestomathy[2], in which the text appeared, he pointed out that it was a regular part of the Ethiopic Bible, where it appears along with the Book of Baruch, the Lamentations of Jeremiah, and the Epistle of Jeremiah[3]. The Ethiopic version is translated from the Greek, and becomes a very important witness for the text. I follow, in my ignorance of Ethiopic, the best translations I can get of Dillmann's text; good ones fortunately are not lacking. There is a German translation by Prätorius in Hilgenfeld's *Zeitschrift für wissenschaftliche Theologie* 1872, p. 230—247: and a later revised translation with notes by König in *Theologische*

---

[1] *Archéologie Orientale*, p. 171.   [2] Lips. 1866.
[3] Cf. Wright, *Cat. of Ethiopic MSS. in the British Museum*; Codd. 7, 8, 14, 16, 20.

Studien und Kritiken for 1877, pp. 318—338. I cite the evidence of this version as *aeth.*

The Menaea for Nov. 4th are a direct authority for the Greek text, which they contain in a somewhat abbreviated form, and in a less pure text. For example the Menaeum printed at Venice in 1843 gives the first five chapters only of the text. The whole of the text, according to Ceriani, is found in the Menaeum printed at Venice in 1609. Ceriani quotes occasionally a MS. Menaeum of the Ambrosian Library; and no doubt the evidence of this class of documents might be multiplied a hundredfold. Their combined evidence is given as *men.*

To this Ceriani added a MS. (marked AF. IX. 31) of the fifteenth century, which he describes as belonging to the Bibliotheca Regia Braidensis; which I take to represent the convent library of the Italian town of Bra in Piedmont. From this MS., with the aid of the Menaeum, Ceriani published the text which appears in the fifth volume of his *Monumenta Sacra* pp. 11—18. This MS. I call *a.*

To these authorities we may add the following from the library of the Patriarchate of Jerusalem.

Cod. *b* = Cod. 34, of the S. Sepulchre portion of the Library, of the eleventh century, containing the Ἐρωτήσεις καὶ Ἀποκρίσεις of Anastasius the Sinaite. At the end there are a number of questions concerning the dissonances of the Evangelists *de resurrectione Christi:* a fragment from Irenæus, the same as is printed in Tischendorf's *Anecdota Sacra et Profana* p. 120 from Cod. Coislin. 120; and on f. 251, at the end of the life of Jeremiah the prophet, comes the title τὰ παραλειπόμενα Ἰερεμίου τοῦ προφητοῦ.

Cod. *c* = Cod. 6 S. Sepulcri of the tenth century has been collated with the foregoing. It contains a valuable text which often deviates widely from that of the foregoing MS. The text begins on f. 242 of the MS.

The next two manuscripts belong to a totally different recension; but they are related *inter se:* the text which they give is an epitome of the Paralipomena, probably taken from the Menaea with appendices from collateral sources: they are as follows:

Cod. *d* = Cod. 66 S. Sep. a late MS. (15th cent.?) containing a collection of apocryphal matters of all kinds: a brief summary may be useful. It begins with an extract from Chrysostom, followed by

f. 6 b. Τοῦ ἁγίου ἀποστόλου καὶ εὐαγγελιστοῦ Ἰωάννου τοῦ

θεολόγου λόγος περὶ τῆς κοιμήσεως τῆς ὑπερευλογημένης καὶ ἐνδόξου δεσποίνης ἡμῶν θεοτόκου καὶ ἀειπαρθένου Μαρίας.

f. 14. Τῆς σεβασμίας μεταστάσεως τῆς ὑπερενδόξου δεσποίνης ἡμῶν καὶ ἀειπαρθένου.

f. 23. Περίοδοι τοῦ ἁγίου καὶ ἐνδόξου ἀποστόλου καὶ εὐαγγελιστοῦ παρθένου ἐπιστηθίου φίλου Ἰωάννου τοῦ θεολόγου.

f. 93 b. Πράξεις τοῦ ἁγίου καὶ ἐνδόξου καὶ πανευφήμου ἀποστόλου Θωμᾶ.

f. 109 b. Ἐκ τῶν περιόδων τοῦ ἁγίου καὶ ἐνδόξου ἀποστόλου Φιλίππου. ὑπὸ (l. ἀπὸ) πράξεως πέντε καὶ δεκάτου μέχρι τέλους τοῦ μαρτυρίου αὐτοῦ.

f. 124. Πράξεις Ματθία καὶ Ἀνδρέα ἐν τῇ χώρᾳ τῶν ἀνθρωποφάγων.

f. 146 b. Πράξεις τῶν ἀποστόλων Πέτρου καὶ Παύλου καὶ πῶς ἐν Ῥώμῃ ἐμαρτύρησαν ἐπὶ Νέρωνος.

f. 165. Μαρτύριον τοῦ ἁγίου ἀποστόλου καὶ εὐαγγελιστοῦ Μάρκου.

f. 169 b. Τοῦ ἁγίου ἀποστόλου καὶ εὐαγγελιστοῦ Λουκᾶ.

f. 177. Ὑπόμνησις εἰς τὸν ἅγιον ἀπόστολον καὶ εὐαγγελιστὴν Ματθαῖον.

f. 181 b. Τοῦ ἁγίου ἐνδόξου ἀποστόλου Ἰακώβου ἀδελφοῦ τοῦ ἁγίου Ἰωάννου τοῦ θεολόγου.

f. 182. Διήγησις περὶ τῆς ἀντιλογίας τοῦ διαβόλου μετὰ τοῦ κυρίου ἡμῶν Ἰησοῦ Χριστοῦ.

f. 186. Βίος σύντομος καὶ πολιτεία τοῦ ὁσίου πατρὸς ἡμῶν Ἰωάννου τοῦ ἐν τῷ φρέατι.

f. 188 b. Βίος τοῦ ἁγίου Γερασίμου.

f. 190 b. Διήγησις Μάλχου μοναχοῦ.

f. 194. Διήγησις περὶ...Νικολάου.

f. 196. Μαρτύριον Μενίγνου (sic).

f. 199. Ἄθλησις...Θεοδώρου.

f. 202 b. Μαρτύριον Φωτείνου.

f. 209 b. Διήγησις...ἐν τῷ βίῳ...Παχωμίου.

f. 212 b. Διήγησις περὶ τοῦ θρήνου τοῦ προφήτου Ἱερεμία περὶ τῆς Ἱερουσαλήμ. καὶ περὶ τῆς ἁλώσεως ταύτης καὶ περὶ τῆς ἐκστάσεως Ἀβιμέλεχ. εὐλόγησον δέσποτα.

A life of Jeremiah is prefixed to the text of the Paralipomena.

f. 215. περὶ τῆς ἁλώσεως Ἱερουσαλήμ· τὰ λαληθέντα ὑπὸ κυρίου πρὸς Ἱερεμίαν· καὶ ὅπως ἡ αἰχμαλωσία γέγονεν ἔχει οὕτως.

f. 222 b. 'Οπτασία Κοσμᾶ μοναχοῦ.

f. 229. Διήγησις ἑτέρας ὀπτασίας.

f. 231 b. Διήγησις περὶ τοῦ γενομένου θαύματος ἐν 'Αφρίκῃ [ἐν] τῇ πόλει Καρταγένῃ.

f. 233. 'Εφραίμ· εἰς τὸν πάγκαλον 'Ιωσήφ.

f. 252. Χρυσοστόμου· εἰς τὸν μάταιον βίον.

f. 260. Διήγησις καὶ διαθήκη τοῦ δικαίου καὶ πατριάρχου 'Αβραάμ· δηλοῖ δὲ καὶ τὴν πεῖραν τοῦ θανάτου αὐτοῦ. εὐλόγησον δέσποτα.

It will be seen that the MS. though late contains a great deal of valuable apocryphal matter: for example, I found it worth while when working at Jerusalem to copy the whole of the 'Αντιλογία τοῦ διαβόλου and the Διαθήκη 'Αβραάμ, as well as the Baruch matter.

The title attached to the Baruch extracts seems to imply that they were taken from a Menaeum.

Cod. e = Cod. 35 S. Crucis (the library of the Convent of the Holy Cross now removed to the Patriarchal Library at Jerusalem). This is also a late paper MS. (xvth cent.) and contains a similar text of the Paralipomena to the preceding. It contains also the prefixed life of Jeremiah. The MS. opens with a διήγησις 'Ιακώβου εἰς τὸ γενέσιον τῆς θεοτόκου. We have collated the Baruch text with Cod. d.

We have thus the following authorities for the text:

aeth = Ethiopic version as edited by Dillmann.
men = The Menaea.
a = Cod. Braidensis.
b = Cod. 34 S. Sepulcri.
c = Cod. 6 S. Sepulcri.
d = Cod. 66 S. Sepulcri.
e = Cod. 35 S. Crucis.

In using these authorities, we find that d and e are only transcripts, with occasional modifications, from the Menaeum; and a very little examination will shew that the text of the Menaeum is only a secondary authority. Of the remaining MSS., a and b present an almost identical text, and constitute together a single authority. The text is thus reduced to three principal authorities, which vary widely *inter se* from time to time; viz. aeth, a + b, and c. In comparing the readings we shall find that the Ethiopic text

is on the whole much superior to the text of *a*, *b*; and that where
it diverges from this, it almost always has *c* associated with it [1].

We should thus be led to take generally the consensus of
aeth and *c* as furnishing the earliest reading; but this would
require, first, that there should be a margin left for occasional
cases in which *a*, *b* may have preserved the right reading: and
second, that the consensus of *a*, *b* with either of the pair *aeth* and
c against the other should be regarded as, almost to a certainty,
the primitive reading.   The MSS. would thus be represented by

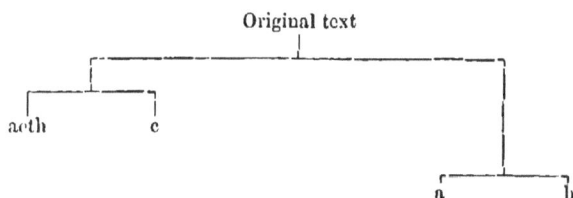

The scheme will test itself readily as we edit the text; but a
few instances may perhaps be taken to shew the relation of the
authorities and the generally corrupt state of transcription.

v. 23.   *a*.   εἰ μὴ ἦς πρεσβύτης, καὶ ὅτι οὐκ ἐξὸν ἀνθρώπῳ Θεοῦ
ὑβρίσαι τὸν μείζονα αὐτοῦ· ἐπεὶ κατεγέλων ὅτι μαίνῃ.

b.   εἰ μὴ εἶς πρεσβύτης· καὶ ὅτι οὐκ ἐξὼν ἀνθρώπῳ Θεοῦ
ὑβρίσαι τὸν μείζονα αὐτοῦ· ἐπεὶ καταγέλων σου καὶ ἔλεγον ὅτι
μένει.

c.   εἰ μὴ εἶς πρεσβύτης· καὶ οὐκ ἐξὼν ἀνθρώπων ὑβρίσαι τὸν
μείζονα αὐτοῦ· ἐπικατεγέλουν σοι καὶ ἔλεγον ὅτι μὲν [ἠχμαλώ-
τευσον κτέ].

aeth.   Wenn du nicht ein bejahrter Mann wärest, so würde ich
dich schmähen und über dich lachen, doch nicht soll es geschehen,
dass man einen Menschen verachtet, und zwar einen bejahrten
Mann; und wenn du nicht ein solcher wärest, so würde ich sagen,
dass du ausser dir bist.

Comparing these readings we see that the Θεοῦ is to be
rejected in *a*, *b*: while the consensus of *b*, *c* and the Ethiopic makes
it certain that the word ἐπικατεγέλων was followed more or less

---

[1] The superiority of the Ethiopic text is affirmed also by König (*Stud. u. Krit.*
1877, p. 319) : "In der That hat mir eine durchgängige Vergleichung beider Texte
gezeigt, dass beide weit von einander abweichen, ja dass der äthiopische dem
Originale der Schrift näher als der bis jetzt veröffentlichte griechische Text steht."

closely by καὶ ἔλεγον; while the similarity of the endings ἐγέλων and ἔλεγον is sufficient reason for the omission of a clause. Nor can we be far wrong if, restoring the particle ἄν from the Menaea, we read ἐπικατεγέλων ἄν σοι καὶ ἔλεγον ὅτι μαίνῃ.

vi. 22. *a.* ὁ ἀκούων, ἀφορίσω αὐτὸν ἐκ τῆς Βαβυλῶνος, ὁ δὲ μὴ ἀκούων, ξένος γένηται τῆς Ἰερουσαλήμ.

b. ὁ ἀκούων, κτέ..

......................γενήσεται κτέ......................

c. ὁ ἀκούων ἀναφέρω αὐτὸν ἐκ τοῦ λάκκου τῆς Βαβυλῶνος· ὁ δὲ μὴ ἀκούων ξένος γίνεται τῆς Ἰερουσαλὴμ καὶ τῆς Βαβυλῶνος.

aeth. Diejenigen, welche (auf sie) gehört haben, werde ich aus Babylon ausführen und sie werden nicht verbannt von Jerusalem in Babylon sein.

The chief point here is the addition of the words 'and from Babylon' by Cod. *c*: they evidently stood in the Ethiopic archetype but being unintelligible they were corrected to 'in Babylon.'

Thus we have the consensus of *c* and *aeth* for an apparently unintelligible reading: but the story explains it, as we proceed, for those who will not obey Jeremiah are not only refused admission to Jerusalem, but they are rejected also on their attempt to return to Babylon. So that the clause is a genuine one.

vii. 12. *a, b.* ἐὰν κυκλώσουσί σε πάντα τὰ πετεινὰ τοῦ οὐρανοῦ καὶ βούλωνται πολεμῆσαι μετὰ σοῦ, ἀγώνισαι· (*b* ἀγώνησαι).

c. ἐὰν κυκλώσωσίν σε πάντα τὰ πετεινὰ τοῦ οὐρανοῦ, καὶ πάντες οἱ ἐχθροὶ τῆς ἀληθείας βουλόμενοι πολεμῖσαι μετὰ σοῦ, ἀγώνισαι.

The missing clause being found also in the Ethiopic, we are entitled to restore it to the text.

There are some places, however, in which the text is extremely obscure in all authorities: and we may even be obliged to resort to conjecture for a reading. For example:

iv. 10. *a, b.* ταῦτα εἰπὼν Βαροὺχ, ἐξῆλθεν ἔξω τῆς πόλεως, κλαίων καὶ λέγων, "Ὅτι διὰ σὲ, Ἰερουσαλήμ, ἐξῆλθον ἀπὸ σοῦ.

c. ταῦτα εἰπὼν, ἐξῆλθεν κλαίων καὶ λέγων, "Ὅτι λοιποῦ διὰ σὲ, Ἰερουσαλήμ· καὶ ἐξῆλθεν ἐκ τῆς πόλεως.

aeth. Und nachdem er dieses geredet hat, ging er weinend hinaus.

Here the Ethiopic has cut the knot of a difficult passage by the simple process of omission of a clause and *a, b* by the omission of a word: we may suggest the reading Ὅτι λυπούμενος διὰ σὲ, Ἰερουσαλὴμ, ἐξῆλθον ἀπὸ σοῦ. This furnishes the necessary material for the explanation of the variants.

vi. 16. *a, b.* Ἀποστείλας δὲ εἰς τὴν διασπορὰν τῶν ἐθνῶν, ἤνεγκεν χάρτην καὶ μέλανα καὶ ἔγραψεν ἐπιστολήν.

c. ὁ δὲ Βαροὺχ ἀπέστειλεν εἰς τὴν ἀγωρὰν (sic!) τῶν ἐθνῶν καὶ ἤνεγκεν χάρτην καὶ μέλαν καὶ ἔγραψεν ἐπιστολήν.

aeth. Und Baruch geleitete ihn bis zur Strasse und holte Papier und Tinte und schrieb.

The Ethiopic text shews that διασπορὰ is a corruption: for it gives *Strasse* which is equivalent in Eastern language to ἀγορά: (e.g. Sûk in Arabic is either *street* or *market;* and this interchangeability of the two words has given rise to variant and conflate readings in the New Testament in Mark vi. 56 ἐν ταῖς ἀγοραῖς καὶ ἐν ταῖς πλατείαις:) so that we may safely read ἀγορά: but ἀγορὰ τῶν ἐθνῶν is more difficult: yet the τῶν ἐθνῶν cannot be omitted since it is found in *c* as well as in *a, b.* Let us see, then, whether there are any considerations that will throw light on this difficult reading. Is there any market that might be called the Gentiles' market; or any street that might bear the name of the Gentiles' street? This question brings before us some very interesting matter. We may establish the following points: (*a*) that there was a famous fair held annually at Abraham's oak near Hebron; (β) that this was especially a fair of the Gentiles; (γ) that this fair is closely connected in history with the Jewish war under Hadrian; and (δ) that the introduction of the city Hebron, and the terebinth of Abraham, into the story was suggested to the writer by the earlier Baruch whom he so largely draws upon in other details. And first, with regard to the fair: Sozomen in his Ecclesiastical History devotes a chapter to the account of the religious disorders that prevailed at this fair, and to the suppression by Constantine of the forms of idolatry that had associated themselves with it. At this Terebinth, says he, there assemble annually the inhabitants of the country and the remoter parts of Palestine, and the Phœnicians and the Arabians, during the summer season to keep a feast, and very many resort thither for the sake of trade, both buyers and sellers. The feast is diligently frequented by all nations, by the Jews because they boast of their descent from Abraham; by the Greeks because angels there appeared to men, and by

Christians. On this famous spot Constantine ordered the erection of a Christian Church[1].

This concourse of the Gentiles at the Terebinth-fair appears also from the *Onomasticon* of Eusebius, who says that the oak and sepulchre of Abraham are an object of religious veneration πρὸς τῶν ἐχθρῶν, where Reland long ago[2] saw that we must correct ἐχθρῶν into ἐθνῶν, as Lagarde has done in his edition of the *Onomasticon*[3].

Sozomen, indeed, speaks of the Jews as frequenting the fair, but there is evidence to set against this statement, according to Jerome[4], who says that "exsecrabile fuisse Judaeis mercatum celeberrimum visere." We may, therefore, call this annual gathering a market of the Gentiles, in agreement with our text of Baruch.

The reason of the detestation which the Jews felt for this fair will be found according to Jerome in the consideration of the connexion between the fair and the Hadrian War. Many thousands of men had been sold at this market, after the capture of Bether, the last stronghold of the Jews, some of them at miserable rates, such as the price of a horse's feed of corn. Thus Jerome says, "quod ultima captivitate sub Hadriano, quando et urbs Jerusalem subversa est, innumerabilis populus diversae aetatis et utriusque sexus in mercato Terebinthi venumdatus sit. Et idcirco exsecrabile etc.," and again in his Commentary on Zechariah[5], "legamus veteres historias et traditiones plangentium Judaeorum, quod in tabernaculo Abrahae, ubi nunc per annos singulos mercatus celeberrimus exercetur, post ultimam eversionem quem sustinuerant ab Hadriano multa hominum millia venumdata sint et quae vendi non potuerint translata in Aegyptum." It is clear, therefore, that the market, however famous, and widely attended, could never have been popular with the Jews. It has even been questioned whether in the time subsequent to the war, they were not disqualified by edict from

---

[1] Sozomen *H. E.* ii. 4, ἐνταῦθα δὲ λαμπρὰν εἰσέτι νῦν ἐτήσιον πανήγυριν ἄγουσιν ὥρᾳ θέρους οἱ ἐπιχωρίοι, καὶ οἱ προσωτέρω Παλαιστινοί, καὶ Φοίνικες καὶ Ἀρράβιοι. Συνίασι δὲ πλεῖστοι καὶ ἐμπορείας ἕνεκα, πωλήσοντες καὶ ἀγοράσοντες.

[2] Reland, *Palestina* pp. 711 sqq. *sub voce* Chebron.

[3] Ἡ δρῦς Ἀβραὰμ καὶ τὸ μνῆμα αὐτόθι θεωρεῖται καὶ θρησκεύεται ἐπιφανῶς πρὸς τῶν ἐχθρῶν. Cf. Jerome, *De situ et nominibus*, *sub voce* Arboc, A cunctis in circuitu gentibus terebinthi locus superstitiose colitur.

[4] Jerome, *Comm. in Jer.* xxxi. 15.

[5] Jerome, *Comm. in Zach.* xi. 4, 5.

coming as near to Jerusalem as Hebron; some persons maintain
that they were absolutely exiled from the soil of Palestine; but
in any case we can see clearly that the market was a foreigners'
market, and that it was closely connected historically with
Hadrian's victories. Indeed it is quite possible that Hadrian
established the fair. Something of the kind seems to be implied
in the statement of the Paschal Chronicle, which under the
date 119 A.D. (!) reports as follows: Ἦλθεν Ἀδριανὸς εἰς Ἱεροσό-
λυμα καὶ ἔλαβεν τοὺς Ἰουδαίους αἰχμαλώτους, καὶ ἀπελθὼν εἰς
τὴν λεγομένην Τερέβινθον προέστησεν πανήγυριν καὶ πέπρακεν
αὐτοὺς εἰς ταγὴν ἵππου ἕκαστον, καὶ τοὺς ὑπολειφθέντας ἔλαβεν
εἰς Γάζαν καὶ ἐκεῖ ἔστησεν πανήγυριν καὶ ἐπώλησεν αὐτούς. καὶ
ἕως τοῦ νῦν ἡ πανήγυρις ἐκείνη λέγεται Ἀδριανή.

There is here some confusion of dates, and it is also a question
whether Hadrian visited Palestine himself or whether he merely
established the fairs at the Terebinth and at Gaza by military
authority; there is, however, reason for believing that the time
of Hadrian is the time to which we must refer the establishment
of these annual gatherings.

It appears then that we may put in a good claim for the
identification of the Gentiles' market, and for the justification of
the difficult reading of our best manuscript.

Nor need we be at all surprised at the allusion to Hebron in
the story: for in the Apocalypse of Baruch, which our writer
follows, we find the very same thing. Baruch goes to Hebron
in search of a theophany or at least of an angelophany. It is the
proper place to look for heavenly visitants[1]. Our Ethiopic Version,
if we could accept its reading, would make the Christian Baruch

[1] The parallelism between the two writers may be seen by placing the passages
side by side:

Apocal. Bar.	Bar. Christ.
xxi. 1. Et abii inde et sedi in Valle Cedron in caverna terrae.	iv. 11. καὶ ἔμεινεν ἐν μνημείῳ καθεζόμενος.
xlvii. Et cum exissem ac dimisissem eos, abii inde et dixi eis; Ecce ego vado usque ad Hebron: illuc enim misit me Fortis.	vi. 16. ὁ δὲ Βαροὺχ ἀποστείλας εἰς τὴν ἀγορὰν τῶν ἐθνῶν ἤνεγκε χάρτην καὶ μέλανα καὶ ἔγραψεν ἐπιστολήν.
lxxvii. 18. Et fuit prima et vigesima mense octavo veni ego Baruch et sedi subtus quercum in umbra ramorum (? is this the Terebinth)...et scripsi has duas epistolas.	

also go to Hebron, as the proper place to finish the interview with the angel. This would bring the two Apocalypses into even closer relation: but we need not assume this. If our supposition be correct that the book belongs to the close of the Hadrian War, it is certain that the thoughts of the writer must have turned to the market where the Jews were sold into slavery; and conversely, if we have properly identified the Gentiles' market, the argument is in favour of referring the book to the time of Hadrian as the most likely period for an allusion to the Terebinth.

These instances, then, will perhaps suffice to shew the nature of the text with which we are dealing. It need scarcely be remarked that a host of insignificant itacisms and cases of corrupt transcription have been neglected. The chapters and verses are taken from the text of Ceriani.

Note on the Geography of Ezra and Baruch.

As we study the parallels between this pair of Apocalypses, or between any pair of the triad, 4 Ezra, Apocal. Baruch, Bar. Christ., we derive great advantage for the interpretation of the three texts. It is a great gain, for instance, to see how much, in each case, depends on a proper knowledge of the suburbs of Jerusalem and the country between that city and Hebron. We will take the matter a little further and try to apply our results to a problem that has been hitherto unsolved. Let us ask ourselves the question whether it is possible to identify the field of Arphad or Ardath mentioned in the 4th book of Ezra as the locality of one of the visions of that Apocalypse. The passage runs "ibis in campum florum ubi domus non est aedificata, et manduces solummodo de floribus campi......et profectus sum, sicut dixit mihi, in campum qui vocatur Arphad et sedi ibi in floribus" (iv. Esd. ix. 24—26). The MSS. are, as might be expected, in the greatest confusion over this Ardath: the Latin texts reading Ardath, Ardat, Ardoch, or Ardach, which are evidently modifications of a primitive Ardlat, or Ardath; the Arabic reads Araat, the Armenian Ardab; while the Syriac and Ethiopic agree in reading Arphad, and the weight of their combined testimony is so great that it is the accepted reading in Fritzsche's text. On the other hand the Arabic reading is very close, when written in uncial Greek, to the Latin reading; nor is the Armenian very far

from it. The question being insoluble from the MSS. alone, we
turn to the known relations between the group of Apocalypses
mentioned above: the first thought that suggests itself is that
perhaps the field in question may be the field of Agrippa mentioned in Christian Baruch. The two names are not so remote
as to render identification impossible, and if we imagine the
γ to drop out we can come very near to the Arphad of the
Syriac version. But perhaps this assumption is a little too
difficult, and so we will try another and easier one.

Observing the fact that Hebron is mentioned in Apocal.
Baruch as one of the seats of prophetic inspiration, and that
Hebron is also implied in the Christian Baruch, we ask ourselves
whether it is mentioned in 4 Ezra. Now if we turn to the
Apocalypse of Baruch, we find that the vision at Hebron is
preceded by a seven days' fast, and that before the prophet begins
his fast or sets out for Hebron he bids farewell to the people and
their elders who are extremely unwilling that he should depart
from amongst them. The parallel to this passage in 4 Ezra is
in c. xii. v. 40—51; as we may see from the following:

Apocal. Bar.	4 Esdras.
c. xlvi. Et responderunt filius meus et seniores populi et dixerunt mihi: Usque ad istiusmodi humiliavit nos Fortis, ut recipiat te a nobis cito et vere erimus in tenebris, &c. &c.	c. xii. 40. Et factum est cum audisset omnis populus quoniam pertransierunt septem dies et ego non fuissem reversus in civitatem et congregant se omnis a minimo usque ad maximum et venit ad me et dixerunt mihi dicentes,
	41. Quid peccavimus tibi et quid iniuste egimus in te...tu enim nobis superasti... sicut lucerna in loco obscuro.
c. xlvii. Et cum exissem ac dimisissem eos abii inde et dixi eis; Ecce ego vado usque ad Hebron...et veni ad eum locum ubi sermo factus fuerat ad me et sedi ibi et ieiunavi septem diebus, et factum est post dies septem....	50. Et profectus est populus sicut dixi ei in civitatem: ego autem sedi in campo septem diebus sicut mihi mandavit et manducavi de floribus, &c. Et factum est post dies septem....

We suspect, then, that the place of the fifth vision of Ezra
(the vision of the great Eagle) may be taken to be Hebron; but
a glance at the text will shew that the scene is the same as in
the fourth vision (the vision of the Sorrowing Woman): and this
scene is the field of Arphad, or Ardath, or whatever may be its
right name. It seems, therefore, that Hebron as a place for
visions turns up in all three Apocalypses, and that Ardath is in

its neighbourhood. With some likelihood we may say further that the oak of Abraham as a place for celestial communications turns up in all three writings: in the Christian Baruch by implication in the allusion to the Gentiles' market or fair at the Terebinth; and in the Apocalypse of Baruch the oak is suggested in the parallel passage to this, quoted in a previous note (Apocal. Bar. c. lxxvii. 18)[1]. But it is also in Ezra, for we find in c. xiii. 57, "Et profectus sum et transii in campum (sc. Ardath)...et sedi ibi tribus diebus. (c. xiv.) Et factum est tertio die, et ego sedebam sub quercu (sc. Terebintho)."

Now observe further that the place of vision is described in Ezra as "campum...ubi domus non est aedificata," and compare the description which Sozomen gives of the sacred oak and its surroundings. "The place is open and cultivated ground, nor are there any buildings except the well and the ancient Abrahamic buildings around the oak" (αἴθριος γὰρ καὶ ἀρόσιμός ἐστιν ὁ χῶρος καὶ οὐκ ἔχων οἰκήματα ἢ μόνα τὰ περὶ τὴν δρῦν πάλαι τοῦ Ἀβραὰμ γενόμενα καὶ τὸ φρέαρ τὸ παρ' αὐτοῦ κατασκευασθέν). At first sight the parallelism of these two passages seems a little artificial; but this objection disappears as soon as we observe that in either case the absence of buildings is a corollary from the sanctity of the place. It had been rendered holy by the Theophany which had occurred there. Each of our three Apocalyptists is occupied with the subject of the Upper Jerusalem, and examination shews that *it was believed that Abraham had seen this Heavenly City at Mamre.* Let us then compare what Ezra and Apocalyptic Baruch say on this point:

Bar. Apocal.	4 Esdras.
iv. 3. "Ostendi eam (sc. Jerusalem) Adamo priusquam peccaret; cum vero abjecit mandatum, sublata est ab eo, ut etiam paradisus. Et postea ostendi eam servo meo Abrahamo noctu inter divisiones victimarum."	x. 50. Ostendit tibi Altissimus claritatem gloriae eius (sc. Jerusalem) et pulchritudinem decoris eius. Propterea enim dixi tibi ut venires in agrum ubi non est fundamentum aedificii; nec enim poterat opus aedificii hominis sustinere in loco ubi incipiebat Altissimi civitas ostendi.

The place of Ezra's vision is the same as that of Abraham.

We have thus proved that the scene of the 14th chapter of Ezra is geographically identified with the neighbourhood of Abraham's oak; if any doubt remained on our mind as to the correctness of

[1] p. 34.

the investigation, it might be dispelled by the following further
consideration : when Ezra is sitting under the oak, a voice comes
to him out of the bush saying, Ezra, Ezra; and the speaker goes
on to say that it was in the burning bush that he appeared to
Moses when the people was in bondage in Egypt. Now we may
very well ask, What is the reason for this abrupt allusion to the
burning bush ; how came the author's mind to travel that way?
The answer is that the Terebinth of Mamre was supposed to have
the same virtue of non-inflammability as the bush in Mount Sinai.
The evidence for this will be found in Reland, *Palestina*, under
the heading Chebron, and is as follows:

Ps. Eustathius, writing a commentary on the *Hexaemeron*,
says (Migne, *Patr. Gr.* xviii. 778) that Joseph was buried in the
same place as his ancestor Abraham, and that in this place is
the Terebinth where Jacob hid the idols of Laban, and which is
still reverenced by the people of the neighbouring countries....
And if this Terebinth be set on fire it is swallowed in flame and
one would think it to have been consumed; but as soon as the
fire is extinguished the Terebinth is seen to be unharmed. The
same account is given by Georgius Syncellus in his *Chronographia*
(ed. Niebuhr, Vol. I. 202): and it appears that Syncellus and
Eustathius are drawing from a common authority, since their
language is similar, and they both make the mistake of confound-
ing the oak at Shechem with the tree at Mamre. This common
authority is named by Syncellus; it is the chronographer Julius
Africanus, who must therefore be also responsible for the blunder[1].

---

[1] We give the passages side by side :

Ps. Eustathius.

Ἐπὶ τέλει δὲ καὶ τὸν Ἰωσήφ, τῆς Αἰγύπτου ἀποχωρήσαντες, κηδείοισιν ἔνθα ὁ προ-
πάτωρ αὐτῶν Ἀβραὰμ προκεκήδευτο· ἐν ᾧ
τόπῳ ὑπῆρχε καὶ ἡ τερέβινθος, ἐφ' ᾗ
ἔκρυψεν Ἰακὼβ τῆς (sic) Λάβαν τὰ εἴδωλα,
ἥτις ἔτι καὶ νῦν εἰς τιμὴν τῶν προγόνων ὑπὸ
τῶν πλησιοχώρων θρησκεύεται· ἔστι γὰρ
ἄχρι τοῦ δεῦρο παρὰ τὸν πρέμνον αὐτῆς
βωμός, ἐφ' ὃν τά τε ὁλοκαυτώματα καὶ τὰς
ἑκατόμβας ἀνέφερον· εἶναί τε φασὶ ῥάβδον
αὐτὴν ἑνὸς τῶν ἐπιξενωθέντων ἀγγέλων
τῷ Ἀβραάμ, ἥνπερ τῷ τόπῳ τότε παρὼν
ἐνεφύτευσε καὶ ἐξ αὐτῆς ἡ ἀξιάγαστος ἀνε-
φύη τερέβινθος. Ὑφαφθεῖσα γὰρ ὅλη πῦρ

Georgius Syncellus.

Ἡ ποιμενικὴ σκήνη τοῦ Ἰακὼβ ἐν Ἐδέσῃ
σωζομένη κατὰ τοὺς χρόνους Ἀντωνίνου
Ῥωμαίων βασιλέως διεφθάρη κεραυνῷ ὥς
φησιν ὁ Ἀφρικανός, ἕως τῶν χρόνων αὐτοῦ
Ἀντωνίνου ἱστόρησας. Ἰακὼβ ἀπαρεσθεὶς
τοῖς ὑπὸ Συμεὼν καὶ Λευὶ πραχθεῖσιν ἐν
Σικίμοις διὰ τὴν τῆς ἀδελφῆς φθορὰν εἰς
τοὺς ἐπιχωρίους, θάψας ἐν Σικίμοις οὓς
ἐφέρετο θεοὺς παρὰ τὴν πέτραν ὑπὸ τὴν
θαυμάσιαν τερέβινθον ἥτις μέχρι νῦν εἰς
τιμὴν πατριαρχῶν ὑπὸ τῶν πλησιοχώρων
τιμᾶται, μετῆρεν εἰς Βαιθήλ· ταύτης παρὰ
πρέμνον βωμὸς ἦν, ὥς φασιν ὁ Ἀφρικανός,
τῆς τερεβίνθου, ἐφ' ὃν τὰς ἐκτενὰς ἀνέφερον

We have thus a perfect explanation of the allusion made by Ezra to the burning bush. There was a tradition that the Terebinth was incombustible. It appears, therefore, that we ought to identify the field of Esdras' vision with the neighbourhood of Hebron and the sacred oak. This suggests that we should read *Arbaa*[1] as the name of the field (the ancient name of Hebron being Kiriath-Arba). Writing this in uncial characters, the word easily becomes ΑΡΒΔΔ, from which the *Ardab* of the Armenian is a mere transposition, and Arphad of the Syriac a slight change of two closely related letters. The other variants readily explain themselves in a similar manner.

The Ezra-Baruch legends in the Koran.

We have in the preceding section traced the process of corruption by which the manuscripts of the fourth book of Ezra have disguised the writer's geography almost beyond identification. We will now add something further to the subject, though only in a tentative manner, by trying to demonstrate that traces of our group of Apocalypses or at least of some of them are to be found in the Koran and in Commentaries on the Koran.

The second chapter of the Koran entitled 'the Cow' contains near the close a curious passage which Sale renders as follows: "Hast thou not considered how he behaved himself who passed by a city which had been destroyed even to her foundations? He said, How shall God quicken this city after she hath been dead? And God caused him to die for an hundred years and afterwards raised him to life. And God said, How long hast thou tarried here? He answered, A day or a part of a day. God said, Nay thou hast tarried here an hundred years. Now look on thy food and drink, they are not yet corrupted; and look on thine ass: and this have we done that we might make thee a sign unto them." And Sale remarks that it is the opinion of the Arabic commentators

γίνεται καὶ νομίζεται τοῖς πᾶσιν εἰς κόνιν ἐκ τῆς φλογὸς ἀναλύεσθαι, καίτοι σβεσθεῖσα μέντοι ἀσινὴς ὅλη καὶ ἀκέραιος δείκνυται.

ἐν ταῖς πανηγύρεσι τῆς χώρας ἔνοικοι, ἡ δ' οὐ κατεκαίετο δοκοῦσα πίπρασθαι. παρὰ ταύτην ὁ τάφος Ἀβραὰμ καὶ Ἰσαάκ. φασὶ δέ τινες ῥάβδον εἶναί τινος τῶν ἐπιξενωθέντων ἀγγέλων τῷ Ἀβραὰμ φυτευθεῖσαν αὐτόθι.

[1] The LXX give uniformly Arboc, which Jerome corrects to *Arbee*: "corrupte in nostris codicibus Arboc scribitur cum in Hebraeis legatur Arbee"

that the person spoken of here is Ozair or Ezra. He gives some
further expansion of the legends, which it is quite likely that he
took from Maracci. At all events there is in this author's *Pro-
dromus ad Refutationem Alcorani* Pt. iv. 85 a good note on the
subject, as follows: "Conveniunt omnes, quos videre potui, Alco-
ranum hic loqui de Ozair, id est Ezra, qui transiens iuxta civitatem
Jerusalem iam a Chaldacis destructam, insidens asino cum canistro
ficorum et cyatho pleno musto, coepit ambigere, quomodo posset
Deus illam urbem restituere, et habitatores eius in ea exstinctos
suscitare. Deus autem mori fecit eum, mansitque mortuus per
centum annos; post quos suscitatus a Deo, vidit ficus et musti
cyathum adhuc integros et incorruptos; asinum vero extinctum
et in ossa redactum: ad quae respiciens Ezra iussu Dei vidit illa
elevari, atque inter se compacta carne vestiri, et fieri asinum, in
quem cum Deus spiritum immisisset statim coepit rudere." D'Herbelot in his *Bibliothèque Orientale*, under the heading *Ozair*, gives
the same traditions more at length: "Les interprètes de l'Alcoran
disent sur ce passage que l'homme dont il est parlé ici est Ozair
ou Esdras lequel ayant été mené in captivité par Bakht-al-Nassar
ou Nabuchodonosor à Babylone, et delivré ensuite miraculeuse-
ment de sa prison, se transporte à Jerusalem, qui étoit pour lors
ruinée, et s'arrêta à un village, fort proche de cette ville, nommé
Sair abad, maison de promenade, et *Deir anab*, lieu de vignoble,
une vigne dans la signification que les Italiens donnent à ce mot.
Ce lieu qui n'étoit couvert que de mazures, avoit cependant dans
son terroir des Figuiers et des Vignes chargez de fruits. Esdras
en prit pour sa provision et alla se loger auprès de quelque pan de
muraille qui restoit encore sur pied. Ce fut là qu'il établit un
hermitage où il vivoit des fruits qu'il avoit cueillis et tenoit un
asne que luy avait servi de monture pendant son voyage, attaché
auprès de luy. Ce saint homme en considerant de ce lieu là les
ruines de la ville Sainte pleuroit amèrement devant le Seigneur et
disoit souvent en luy même, plûtost en admirant la puissance de
Dieu, qu'en murmurant contre elle: 'Comment les ruines de
Jerusalem, pourroient-elles jamais se relever.' Mais il n'eût pas
plûtost conceu cette pensée que Dieu le fit mourir sur le champ et
le tint caché aux yeux de hommes avec tout ce qu'il avoit autour
de lui, l'espace d'un siècle entier, au même état qu'il se trouvoit
pour lors. Cependant, soixante et dix ans après la mort de
Nabuchodonosor, Dieu suscita Noschek Roy de Perse, qui ordonna

le rétablissement de la Ville et du Temple de Jerusalem, et trente ans après les ordres de ce Roy ayant été executez Dieu resuscita Esdras en un tel état qu'il luy parut n'avoir dormi que pendant un jour, mais ayant ouvert les yeux, il connut bientôt, que Dieu avoit operé un grand miracle en sa personne, et s'écria aussitôt, Dieu certainement est tout puissant; car, il peut faire tout ce qu'il luy plait."

Upon the passage which we have quoted from the Koran, Maracci endeavours to shew that the legend, though it contains more figments than words, agrees better with the history of Nehemiah than Ezra; the cup of wine being a reminiscence of the office which Nehemiah held at the Persian court, and the ass a reflection of the beast on which he made the circuit of the ruined city. But he asks in despair " Whence the death of Nehemiah and his ass: and their resurrection after the lapse of a century; and whence this story of the marvellous conservation of wine and figs? Some persons say that it is not Ezra, nor Nehemiah, but a certain *Alchedrum*." The story certainly is a queer confusion of legends; it must be evident that we have many single gentlemen rolled into one, and that the principal one amongst them is our friend Abimelech the Ethiopian, whose basket of figs furnishes the explanation which Maracci searched the Scriptures for in vain.

The mythical Alchedrum is therefore Abimelech: and the sentence in which God directs the supposed Ezra to look on his marvellously conserved food and drink has its origin in the passage where the old man tells Abimelech to look into the basket and see that the figs have no evil smell though they were gathered 66 years ago. We may, if we please, refer the story of the ass and the wine-cup to Nehemiah, but as we have here a practically certain origin for the Mohammedan legends, it is best to exhaust this source before seeking a second, and we find that the story of the sleep of Abimelech is the origin of the one hundred years' death-sleep of the Ezra of the Koran. And indeed although the Koran gives the time as 100 years, the legends quoted by D'Herbelot shew traces of a knowledge of the number 70 as given in corrected copies of the Christian Baruch. Why else should it have been said that the 100 years was made up of 70 years from the death of Nebuchadnezzar together with 30 years to the time of Noschek, king of Persia?

Further, the passage in the Koran is used to prove the re-surrection of the dead by the resurrection of the city. And it is to be noticed that Abimelech when he sees that the figs exude still their milky juice, breaks into an exultant apostrophe to his flesh which God is able to revive.

The writer, too, who made his Ezra sleep 100 years and think it to be a day or part of a day, is in exact consonance with Abimelech who thinks he has slept a very little and would in fact like to sleep a little more.

But, as we have said, the legends collected in D'Herbelot are not totally explained by the introduction of our Abimelech. It looks as if the fourth book of Ezra were here, if not some biblical allusion also to Nehemiah. The account which he gives of Ezra finding a hermitage in a desolate spot not far from the city, is marvellously like the story of the sojourn in the Field of Arphad; his diet of figs may be only a correction for the flowers which Ezra is directed to live on. And even the allusion to the ruins which covered the ground may be an adaptation of Ezra's note that the spot was clear of buildings. We will even go so far as to suspect that the field of Arbaa (Arbad) underlies the per-plexing names which D'Herbelot quotes for the place of Ezra's hermitage.

It seems, therefore, to sum up, that there is good reason to believe that Mohammed was acquainted with the Christian Baruch, and that the Commentators who explained his allusion were acquainted also with the fourth book of Ezra. In view of the uncertainty which prevails with regard to the literary sources of Mohammedanism especially on the Christian side, it may be not wholly useless to have given some confirmation of the theory of Ceriani, that the second chapter of the Koran draws on the story contained in the last words of Baruch.

The Christian Baruch, 4 Ezra, and Barnabas.

An interesting question arises in one passage of our author as to the possibility of a reference to the epistle of Barnabas, and the subject is important enough in view of the uncertainty of the date of that epistle; so that it seems hardly fair to dismiss the matter in the compass of a foot-note.

In c. ix. 15, we find a prediction that the tree of life which is planted in the midst of Paradise will come into the world, and that this tree will cause the fruitless trees to become fruitful, and the boastful trees to wither; and the tree which is established will make them to bend. So at least we have edited, deserting the reading of our MSS.: which give the sense 'will make them to be judged.' The difference between the two readings is only a single letter. Our best MS. has failed here, and the text of the Ethiopic version is so confused, that it is almost unintelligible. That our emendation, however, is substantially correct may be seen from the following passage quoted in Gregory of Nyssa amongst a number of Testimonies against the Jews[1]:

Καὶ τότε ταῦτα συντελεσθήσεται, λέγει Κύριος, ὅταν ξύλον ξύλων (l. ξύλῳ) κλιθῇ καὶ ἀναστῇ καὶ ὅταν ἐκ ξύλου αἷμα στάξει (l. στάξῃ). The two corrections which we have given in brackets, obvious enough of themselves, are given by Ceriani from an Ambrosian MS.[2]

Now this bending of tree to tree is exactly what is spoken of in our author, when he intimates that the tree of life will make all the other trees to bow before it. So that our correction of the text is justified, as we shall see more clearly as we proceed.

Two questions then arise, first as to the origin of the quotation which Nyssen makes: second as to the meaning of the similar matter in the text of our author. We will take these points in order. The passage is very like one in the twelfth chapter of Barnabas, which runs as follows: Ὁμοίως πάλιν περὶ τοῦ σταυροῦ ὁρίζει ἐν ἄλλῳ προφήτῃ λέγοντι· Καὶ πότε ταῦτα συντελεσθήσεται; λέγει Κύριος· ὅταν ξύλον κλιθῇ καὶ ἀναστῇ καὶ ὅταν ἐκ ξύλου αἷμα στάξῃ.

We may regard it as almost certain that Gregory Nyssen is quoting from Barnabas; the differences being so slight that we can at once allow for them by the ordinary processes of transcription. We have only to imagine the text of Barnabas to have dropped ξύλῳ after ξύλον and all is clear. But this brings

---

[1] Zacagni, *Collectanea Monumenta*, p. 309; Ceriani, *Mon. Sac.* v. i. 108.
[2] Cod. C. 135, Inf.

Barnabas into very close relation with the language of the Christian Baruch.

We must not, however, assume any direct quotation between them, inasmuch as the passage in Barnabas is distinctly given as a quotation from one of the prophets. Nor should we have much difficulty in identifying this prophet with the Apocalyptic Ezra, because a great part of the quotation can at once be found in his text, and because the Christian Baruch, who exhibits parallel language to that part of Barnabas' quotation which cannot be found in the text of Ezra as edited, has been shewn to have internal relations with the fourth book of Ezra. We will place the passages side by side for the sake of comparison :

Gregory Nyss., and Barnabas (xii. 1).	Christian Baruch (ix. 15, 16).	4 Ezra iv. 33, v. 5, 9.
Καὶ πότε ταῦτα συντελεσθήσεται ; λέγει Κύριος· Ὅταν ξύλον κλιθῇ καὶ ἀναστῇ καὶ ὅταν ἐκ ξύλου αἷμα στάξῃ.	Γίνεται δὲ μετὰ τοὺς καιροὺς τούτους, καὶ ἔρχεται εἰς τὴν γῆν τὸ δένδρον τῆς ζωῆς τὸ ἐν μέσῳ τοῦ παραδείσου φυτευθέν, ... καὶ τὰ βεβλαστηκότα καὶ μεγαλαυχοῦντα..................... ποιήσει κλιθῆναι τὸ δένδρον τὸ στηριχθέν........................ .... τὰ γλυκέα ὕδατα ἁλμυρὰ γενήσονται.	Et respondi et dixi, Quomodo et quando haec?...... .... et de ligno sanguis stillabit, et lapis dabit vocem suam .... et in dulcibus aquis salsae invenientur.

We must then, I think, conclude that the Recension of 4 Ezra which Barnabas and the Christian Baruch used contained a clause answering to ὅταν ξύλον ξύλῳ κλιθῇ. This is, I think, the very conclusion arrived at by Le Hir in his discussion of the fourth book of Ezra[1]. Le Hir, however, goes further and very ingeniously seeks the origin of the whole Ezra passage in the prophet Habakkuk, where the stone cries from the wall that is builded by deceit and the cross-beam answers back to it, and where woe is denounced on those who build houses by blood. The conjunction of stone, tree and blood is suggestive even in a translation, especially when it is a talking stone, too, as in 4 Ezra and in the later Baruch. But M. Le Hir goes so far as to restore the whole passage of Habakkuk into close textual agreement with Barnabas and Ezra, as the following will shew:

---

[1] Études Bibliques, p. 198.

Habakkuk ii. 11.

כפיס מעץ יעננה: הוי בנה עיר בדמים וכונן...

Suggested corruption of Le Hir,

כפיס מעץ יענה ויעיר: בדם ימוך

Now without endorsing the whole of the suggestions of this
reading, we may say that the first one, which turns on the equiva-
lence of the two Hebrew roots which mean respectively *to answer*
and *to bend*, is so striking that we may be pretty sure we have
tracked the quotations to their source; and we may add to this,
what I do not think Le Hir noted, that the words which precede in
Habakkuk "the stone shall cry out of the wall," answer exactly to
"the stone shall give its voice" of Ezra, and, in fact, furnish the
momentum for the misunderstandings which culminate in the
personification of the dying Jeremiah by a stone. We may therefore follow with confidence the greater part of Le Hir's reasoning.

And, bearing in mind that the Hebrew text of the passage in
Habakkuk is perfectly satisfactory, and needs neither textual correction nor any subtleties of interpretation, we may say that in
a certain circle, probably Jerusalem, there prevailed a flagrant
corruption or mistranslation of the passage: that this corruption
became the basis of exegetical subtleties on the part of Apocryphal
writers, both Jews and Christians: the former, probably, explained
the 'blood that drops from wood' of the martyrdom of Isaiah:
while the latter, who never missed the chance of seeing the 'cross'
in any reference to 'beams,' 'trees,' 'rods' or 'timber,' were able
to find a prophetic testimony to the central object of their faith in
the fact that 'wood should bend to wood,' or that 'blood should
trickle' therefrom.

And this brings us to the second point; viz. the meaning which
our Christian Baruch attached to the words which he has absorbed.
He is preaching the triumph of the Cross; this may be regarded to
be as certain as if he had followed Barnabas' example and prefixed a
paragraph saying that the prophet is here speaking of the Cross.
But it is not quite so clear whether he is speaking of the assumption of the Cross, which is of course the Tree of Life, into Paradise
and its adoration by the rest of the trees of the garden, or of the
descent of the Tree from Paradise and its adoration by the rest of
the trees of the world. The former opinion derives some weight
from the fact that some of the early Christians believed the Cross

had been caught up into Paradise, a natural belief when we consider that they had so persistently taught that it was the Tree which had been planted in the midst of the garden.

But the latter opinion agrees better with the statement of the writer that the tree is coming to the earth and that the fruitless trees (i.e. the Gentiles) will under its influence bear fruit, while those that have sprouted and are high-minded (i.e. the extreme section of the Jews) will have to bow before it.

ΤΑ ΠΑΡΑΛΕΙΠΟΜΕΝΑ ΙΕΡΕΜΙΟΥ ΤΟΥ ΠΡΟΦΗΤΟΥ.

I. Ἐγένετο, ἡνίκα ἠχμαλωτεύθησαν οἱ υἱοὶ Ἰσραὴλ ἀπὸ 1
τοῦ βασιλέως τῶν Χαλδαίων, ἐλάλησεν ὁ Θεὸς πρὸς Ἱερεμίαν·
Ἱερεμία, ὁ ἐκλεκτός μου, ἀνάστα, ἔξελθε ἐκ τῆς πόλεως
ταύτης, σὺ καὶ Βαρούχ· ἐπειδὴ ἀπολῶ αὐτὴν διὰ τὸ πλῆθος
τῶν ἁμαρτιῶν τῶν κατοικούντων ἐν αὐτῇ. Αἱ γὰρ προσευχαὶ 2
ὑμῶν ὡς στῦλος ἑδραῖός ἐστιν ἐν μέσῳ αὐτῆς, καὶ ὡς τεῖχος
ἀδαμάντινον περικυκλοῦν αὐτήν. Νῦν ἀναστάντες ἐξέλθατε 3
πρὸ τοῦ τὴν δύναμιν τῶν Χαλδαίων κυκλῶσαι αὐτήν. Καὶ 4
ἀπεκρίθη Ἱερεμίας, λέγων· Παρακαλῶ σε, Κύριε, ἐπίτρεψόν
μοι τῷ δούλῳ σου λαλῆσαι ἐνώπιόν σου. Εἶπεν δὲ αὐτῷ
ὁ Κύριος· Λάλει, ὁ ἐκλεκτός μου Ἱερεμίας. Καὶ ἐλάλησεν 5
Ἱερεμίας, λέγων· Κύριε παντοκράτωρ, παραδίδως τὴν πόλιν
τὴν ἐκλεκτὴν εἰς χεῖρας τῶν Χαλδαίων, ἵνα καυχήσηται ὁ
βασιλεὺς μετὰ τοῦ πλήθους τοῦ λαοῦ αὐτοῦ, καὶ εἴπῃ ὅτι,
Ἴσχυσα ἐπὶ τὴν ἱερὰν πόλιν τοῦ Θεοῦ ; Μὴ, Κύριέ μου· ἀλλ' 6
εἰ θέλημά σού ἐστιν, ἐκ τῶν χειρῶν σου ἀφανισθήτω. Καὶ 7
εἶπε Κύριος τῷ Ἱερεμίᾳ· Ἐπειδὴ σὺ ἐκλεκτός μου εἶ, ἀνάστα
καὶ ἔξελθε ἐκ τῆς πόλεως ταύτης, σὺ καὶ Βαρούχ· ἐπειδὴ
ἀπολῶ αὐτὴν διὰ τὸ πλῆθος τῶν ἁμαρτιῶν τῶν κατοικούντων

Title, with *abc*; *aeth*, The rest of the words of Baruch.

I. 1 ηνικα *ab*; οτε *c* | οι; *c* om | απο *ab*; υπο *c* | Ιερεμιαν cum *c aeth*; *ab* add
τον προφητην λεγων | Ιερ...Βαρουχ *ab*, *aeth*; αναστηθη και συ και Βαρουχ *c* | απολω
c; απολλω *ab* | αυτην *ab aeth*; την πολιν ταυτην *c* | κατοικουντων *ab*; ενοικουντων *c* |
v. 2 εστιν; *c* om | περικυκλοιν *a*; περικυκλων *b*; περι τα τειχη αυτης *c* (not *aeth*) | *v.* 3 νυν
αναστ. εξελθατε *ab* (*a* εξελθετε); νυν ουν *c*, inserting ανασταντες εξελθατε at the end of
the verse | προ του κτέ following the Menaea and *de*; but *abc* προ του ἡ δυναμις των
χαλδαιων κυκλωσει (κυκλωση *a*) αυτην | *v.* 4 απεκριθη *ab*; ελαλησεν *a* | επιτρεψον μοι *ab*;
κελευσον με *c* | τω δουλω σου *ab*; *c* om | ενωπιον σου *ab*; λογον εναντιον σου *c* | αυτω
c aeth; *ab* om | *v.* 5 ελαλησεν *ab*; ειπεν *c* | λεγων *ab*; om *c* | παραδιδως *a*; παραδιδης *b*;
παραδιδοις *c* | πολιν; *aeth* add ταυτην | μετα...αυτου *ab aeth*; *c* om | *v.* 6 σου (1°); *b*
σον | σου (2'); *c* om | *v.* 7 Κ̄ς; *ab* ο κ̄ς | τω Ιερ. *ab*; προς Ιερεμιαν *c* | αναστα *ab*; αναστηθι
c | εκ...ταυτης *aeth* om | απολω *bc*; *a* om | κατοικ. *ab*; ενοικ. *c* | end of verse *a* adds
απολλω.

8 ἐν αὐτῇ. Οὔτε γὰρ ὁ βασιλεὺς, οὔτε ἡ δύναμις αὐτοῦ, δυνή-
σεται εἰσελθεῖν εἰς αὐτὴν, εἰ μὴ ἐγὼ πρῶτος ἀνοίξω τὰς πύλας
9 αὐτῆς. Ἀνάστηθι οὖν, καὶ ἄπελθε πρὸς Βαροὺχ, καὶ ἀπάγγειλον
10 αὐτῷ τὰ ῥήματα ταῦτα. Καὶ ἀναστάντες ἕκτην ὥραν τῆς
νυκτὸς, ἔλθετε ἐπὶ τὰ τείχη τῆς πόλεως, καὶ δείξω ὑμῖν, ὅτι,
ἐὰν μὴ ἐγὼ πρῶτος ἀφανίσω τὴν πόλιν, οὐ δύιανται εἰσελθεῖν
11 εἰς αὐτήν. Ταῦτα εἰπὼν ὁ Κύριος, ἀπῆλθεν ἀπὸ τοῦ Ἱερεμίου.
1 ΙΙ. Ἱερεμίας δὲ διέρρηξεν τὰ ἱμάτια αὐτοῦ καὶ ἐπέθηκεν
χοῦν ἐπὶ τὴν κεφαλὴν αὐτοῦ· καὶ εἰσῆλθεν εἰς τὸ ἁγιαστήριον
2 τοῦ Θεοῦ· καὶ ἰδὼν αὐτὸν ὁ Βαροὺχ χοῦν πεπασμένον ἐπὶ τὴν
κεφαλὴν αὐτοῦ, καὶ τὰ ἱμάτια αὐτοῦ διερρωγότα, ἔκραξε φωνῇ
μεγάλῃ, λέγων· Πάτερ Ἱερεμία, τί ἔστι σοι, ἢ ποῖον ἁμάρτημα
3 ἐποίησεν ὁ λαός; Ἐπειδὴ ὅταν ἡμαρτάνεν ὁ λαὸς, χοῦν ἔπασσεν
ἐπὶ τὴν κεφαλὴν αὐτοῦ ὁ Ἱερεμίας, καὶ ηὔχετο ὑπὲρ τοῦ λαοῦ,
4 ἕως ἂν ἀφεθῇ αὐτῷ ἡ ἁμαρτία. Ἠρώτησε δὲ αὐτὸν ὁ Βαροὺχ,
5 λέγων· Πάτερ, τί ἔστι σοι ; Εἶπε δὲ αὐτῷ Ἱερεμίας· Φύλαξαι
τοῦ σχίσαι τὰ ἱμάτιά σου, ἀλλὰ σχίσωμεν τὰς καρδίας
ἡμῶν· καὶ μὴ ἀντλήσωμεν ὕδωρ ἐπὶ τὰς ποτίστρας, ἀλλὰ
κλαύσωμεν καὶ γεμίσωμεν αὐτὰς δακρύων· ὅτι οὐ μὴ ἐλεήσῃ
6 τὸν λαὸν τοῦτον ὁ Κύριος. Καὶ εἶπε Βαροὺχ· Πάτερ Ἱερεμία, τί
7 γέγονε; Καὶ εἶπεν Ἱερεμίας ὅτι, Ὁ Θεὸς παραδίδωσι τὴν πόλιν
εἰς χεῖρας τοῦ βασιλέως τῶν Χαλδαίων, τοῦ αἰχμαλωτεῦσαι
8 τὸν λαὸν εἰς Βαβυλῶνα. Ἀκούσας δὲ ταῦτα Βαροὺχ, διέρρηξε
καὶ αὐτὸς τὰ ἱμάτια αὐτοῦ, καὶ εἶπε· Πάτερ Ἱερεμία, τίς σοι
9 ἐδήλωσε τοῦτο ; Καὶ εἶπεν αὐτῷ Ἱερεμίας· Ἔκδεξαι μικρὸν

v. 8 εις ab; προς c | τας π. αυτης ab; αυτοις τας πυλας c | v. 10 δειξω ab; δικνυω c
εαν μη c; εαν μητι ab | αφαν. την πολιν ab aeth; απολεσω αυτην c | πολιν; ab add και
ανοιξω, not c, aeth | διναυνται ab; δυνησονται c | εις αυτην ab; εν αυτη c | v. 11 απηλθεν
ab; ανεχωρησεν c | Ιερ.; c adds εις τον ουνον· not ab aeth.
II. 1 Ιερ...θεου (b)c aeth; ab δραμων δε Ιερεμιας ανηγγειλε τω Βαρουχ ταυτα (b
ταυτα τω Β.) και ελθοντες εις τον ναον του θεου; b adds διερρηξεν τα ιματια αυτου
Ιερεμιας και επεθηκεν χουν επι την κεφαλην αυτου· και ηρξαντο αμφοτεροι κλεειν εν τω
αγιαστηριω του θεου | v. 2 και ιδων ab; ειδων δε c | χουν; c om | αυτου (1ᶜ); c add χουν|
φωνη μεγαλη λεγων a; φωνην μεγαλην λεγ. b; c om | πατερ ab aeth; c om | τι εστιν
ab aeth; απεστην c | εποιησεν ab aeth; ημαρτεν c | v. 3 ημαρτανεν ab aeth; ημαρ-
τεν c | εως αν ab; οπως c | αυτω ab aeth; αυτοις c | αμαρτια; c add αιτη |
v. 4 ερωτησεν ab; επερωτησεν c | αυτον ab; αυτω c | o; c om | πατερ τι εστι σοι c aeth;
τι εστιν τουτο ab | v. 5 τα ιματια σου; c om | αλλα (1ᶜ); ab add μαλλον (not c aeth) | και
(1ᶜ); c om | ποτιστρας; b ποτιστριας | αλλα(2ᶜ); c add μαλλον | τον λαον τ. ο κ. ab; κυρ.
τ. λ. τ. c | v. 6 πατερ Ιερ. ab aeth; προς Ιερεμιαν c | v. 7 Ιερεμιας ab aeth; c om | παρα-
διδωσει a; παραδιδει b; παραδω c | την πολιν ab aeth; c add την εκλεκτην | του βασιλεως
ab aeth; c om | του αιχ. ab; και αρουσι c | v. 8 ταυτα ab aeth; c om | και αυτος ab
(aeth); c om | και ειπεν ab aeth; λεγων c | εδηλωσε ab; απηγγειλεν c.

μετ' ἐμοῦ ἕως ὥρας ἕκτης τῆς νυκτός, ἵνα γνῷς, ὅτι ἀληθές ἐστι
τὸ ῥῆμα. Ἔμειναν οὖν ἐν τῷ θυσιαστηρίῳ κλαίοντες.   10

III. Ὡς δὲ ἐγένετο ἡ ὥρα τῆς νυκτός, καθὼς εἶπεν ὁ Κύριος 1
τῷ Ἰερεμίᾳ, ἦλθον ὁμοῦ ἐπὶ τὰ τείχη τῆς πόλεως Ἰερεμίας καὶ
Βαρούχ. Καὶ ἐγένετο φωνὴ σάλπιγγος, καὶ ἐξῆλθον ἄγγελοι 2
ἐκ τοῦ οὐρανοῦ, κατέχοντες λαμπάδας ἐν ταῖς χερσὶν αὐτῶν,
καὶ ἔστησαν ἐπὶ τὰ τείχη τῆς πόλεως. Ἰδόντες δὲ αὐτοὺς 3
Ἰερεμίας καὶ Βαρούχ, ἔκλαυσαν, λέγοντες· Νῦν ἐγνώκαμεν ὅτι
ἀληθές ἐστι τὸ ῥῆμα. Παρεκάλεσε δὲ Ἰερεμίας τοὺς ἀγγέλους, 4
λέγων· Παρακαλῶ ὑμᾶς μὴ ἀπολέσθαι τὴν πόλιν ἄρτι, ἕως
ἂν λαλήσω πρὸς Κύριον ῥῆμα. Καὶ εἶπεν Κύριος τοῖς ἀγγέλοις·
Μὴ ἀπολέσητε τὴν πόλιν ἕως ἂν λαλήσω πρὸς τὸν ἐκλεκτόν
μου Ἰερεμίαν. Καὶ εἶπε· Δέομαι, Κύριε, κέλευσόν με λαλῆσαι
ἐνώπιόν σου. Καὶ εἶπε Κύριος· Λάλει, ὁ ἐκλεκτός μου Ἰερεμίας. 5
Καὶ εἶπεν Ἰερεμίας· Ἰδοὺ νῦν, Κύριε, ἐγνώκαμεν ὅτι παραδίδως 6
τὴν πόλιν σου εἰς χεῖρας τῶν ἐχθρῶν αὐτῆς, καὶ ἀπαροῦσι τὸν
λαὸν εἰς Βαβυλῶνα. Τί ποιήσωμεν τὰ ἅγιά σου ἢ τὰ σκεύη τῆς 7
λειτουργίας σου, τί θέλεις αὐτὰ ποιήσωμεν; Καὶ εἶπεν αὐτῷ ὁ 8
Κύριος· Ἆρον αὐτά, καὶ παράδος αὐτὰ τῇ γῇ καὶ τῷ θυσιαστηρίῳ
λέγων, Ἄκουε, γῆ, τῆς φωνῆς τοῦ κτίσαντός σε ἐν τῇ περιουσίᾳ
τῶν ὑδάτων, ὁ σφραγίσας σε ἐν ἑπτὰ σφραγῖσιν, ἐν ἑπτὰ και-
ροῖς, καὶ μετὰ ταῦτα λήψῃ τὴν ὡραιότητά σου· φύλαξον τὰ
σκεύη τῆς λειτουργίας ἕως τῆς συνελεύσεως τοῦ ἠγαπημένου.

v. 9 το ρημα bc aeth; ab add τουτο | ουν c aeth; ab add αμφοτεροι | at the end
ab add και ησαν διερρωγοτα τα ιματια αυτων και η γη επι τας κεφαλας αυτων.
III. 1 ως ab; οτε c | της νυκτος ab aeth; c om | Ιερ. και Βαρ. ab; c aeth om | at
end aeth adds und setzen sich nieder indem sie warteten | v. 2 και ιδου a; και aeth; c
om | εγενετο c om | σαλπιγγος c aeth; σαλπιγγων ab | και (2ˀ); c om | αγγ.; c οι
αγγ. | κατεχοντες; c εχοντες | εν τ. χ. αυτων ab aeth; c om | επι ab; εις c | της
πολεως ab aeth; c om | v. 3 λεγοντες c aeth; και ειπαν ab | εγνωκαμεν ab | εγνωμεν c |
v. 4 πολιν; c adds ταυτην (not ab aeth) | προς κ. ρ. c aeth; μετα του θῦ του υψιστου
ab | και ειπ...Ιερεμιαν c aeth; ab om | και ειπε (2ˀ); ab add κλαιων; c om | δεομαι...Ιερ.
(v. 5) ab aeth; c om | v. 6 Κυριε; c om | εγνωκαμεν ab; εγνωμεν c | παραδιδως a; παρα-
διδης b; παραδιδοις c | σου; c om | των εχθρων αυτης ab aeth; των Χαλδαιων c | απαρουσι;
c αρουσιν | v. 7 text as in c (aeth); ab τι θελεις ποιησω τα αγια σκευη της λειτουργιας
v. 8 αυτω ο; c om | αρον ab aeth; αρατε c | παραδος ab aeth; παραδοτε c | και τω θυσ.
c aeth (dem Erdboden und dem Hause des Heiligtums); ab om | λεγων ab aeth; c
om | ακ. γη; οτι γη ακ. c | της φωνης ab (aeth); c om | εν τη π. τ. υδ. ab (aeth durch
die Kraft der Gewässer); c ο πλασας σε εν ουσια των κτισματων | ο σφρ. σε; e men
του σφραγισαντος σε | εν επ. σφρ. ab aeth; c om | εν επ. κ. ab (c καιδροις); aeth
om | και; c om | ληψη τ. ωρ. σου ab (aeth); λημψη την οδον τη ωραιοτητι σου c |
φυλαξον; c και φυλαξης | de men aeth εως της συνελευσεως τ. η; εως της συντελειας τ.
η. ab; c εως ερωτησιν ποιηση κς περι αυτων· οτι ημεις ουκ ευρεθημεν αξιοι φυλαξαι

9 Καὶ ἐλάλησε Ἱερεμίας· Παρακαλῶ σε, Κύριε· δεῖξόν μοι, τὶ ποι-
ήσω Ἀβιμέλεχ τῷ Αἰθίοπι· ὅτι πολλὰς εὐεργεσίας ἐποίησε τῷ
λαῷ καὶ τῷ δούλῳ σου Ἱερεμίᾳ· ὅτι αὐτὸς ἀνέσπασέ με
ἐκ τοῦ λάκκου τοῦ βορβόρου· καὶ οὐ θέλω αὐτὸν, ἵνα ἴδῃ
τὸν ἀφανισμὸν τῆς πόλεως καὶ τὴν ἐρήμωσιν· ἀλλ' ἵνα
10 μὴ λυπηθῇ. Καὶ εἶπε Κύριος τῷ Ἱερεμίᾳ· Ἀπόστειλον
αὐτὸν εἰς τὸν ἀμπελῶνα τοῦ Ἀγρίππα διὰ τοῦ ὄρους· καὶ ἐγὼ
σκεπάσω αὐτὸν, ἕως οὗ ἐπιστρέψω τὸν λαὸν εἰς τὴν πόλιν.
11 Εἶπε δὲ Κύριος τῷ Ἱερεμίᾳ· Ἄπελθε μετὰ τοῦ λαοῦ σου
εἰς Βαβυλῶνα, καὶ μεῖνον μετ' αὐτῶν εὐαγγελιζόμενος αὐτοῖς,
12 ἕως οὗ ἐπιστρέψω αὐτοὺς εἰς τὴν πόλιν. Κατάλειψον δὲ
13 τὸν Βαροὺχ ὧδε, ἕως οὗ λαλήσω αὐτῷ. Ταῦτα εἰπὼν ὁ
14 Κύριος, ἀνέβη ἀπὸ Ἱερεμίου εἰς τὸν οὐρανόν. Ἱερεμίας δὲ
καὶ Βαροὺχ εἰσῆλθον εἰς τὸ ἁγιαστήριον, καὶ τὰ σκεύη
τῆς λειτουργίας παρέδωκαν τῇ γῇ, καθὼς ἐλάλησεν αὐτοῖς ὁ
Κύριος· καὶ αὔθωρον κατέπιεν αὐτὰ ἡ γῆ· ἐκάθισαν δὲ οἱ δύο,
15 καὶ ἔκλαυσαν. Πρωΐας δὲ γενομένης, ἀπέστειλεν Ἱερεμίας
τὸν Ἀβιμέλεχ, λέγων· Ἆρον τὸν κόφινον, καὶ ἄπελθε εἰς
τὸ χωρίον τοῦ Ἀγρίππα διὰ τῆς ὁδοῦ τοῦ ὄρους, καὶ ἐνεγκὼν
ὀλίγα σῦκα, δίδου τοῖς νοσοῦσι τοῦ λαοῦ· ὅτι ἐπὶ σὲ ἡ εὐφρασία
16 τοῦ Κυρίου, καὶ ἐπὶ τὴν κεφαλήν σου ἡ δόξα. Αὐτὸς δὲ ἀπελή-
λυθεν καθὼς εἶπεν αὐτῷ.

1 IV. Πρωΐας δὲ γενομένης, ἰδοὺ ἡ δύναμις τῶν Χαλδαίων
ἐκύκλωσε τὴν πόλιν· ἐσάλπισεν δὲ ὁ μέγας ἄγγελος, λέγων·

αυτας (sic! shewing that the scribe has wandered to c. IV. v. 4) οτι επιτροποι του
ψευδους ευρεθημεν.

v. 9 και ελαλ. ab; ελ. δε c; ab add κλαιων (not c aeth) | Ιερεμιας; c add προς
κν λεγων | παρακαλω; ab add και δυσωπω | τω λαω και τω δ. σου c aeth; ab
om | Ιερεμια: aeth adds weit mehr als alle Leute der Stadt | οτι αυτος ανεσπασεν
ab; c αυτος γαρ ανεστησεν | του βορβορου c aeth; ab om | αυτον ινα ιδη ab aeth;
ινα αφης αυτον ιδειν c | τον αφαν. ab aeth; την ερημωσιν c | πολεως; ab add ταυτης | και
τ. ερ.; c η τον αφανισμον η την ερημωσιν | αλλ ινα μη λυπηθη aeth; ab αλλ ινα ελεησης
αυτον και μη λυπ.: c ηδη (sic) και λυπηθη | v. 10 τω Ιερ.; c om | αμπελωνα; c αγρον | δια
του ορους και εγω c aeth; ab και εν τη σκια του ορους | εως ου επι. ab; c εως αποστρεψω |
εις την πολιν ab aeth; c εις Βαβυλωνα | v. 11; c om | v. 12; c om; aeth om εως ου
λαλ. αυτω | v. 13; c λαλησας δε αυτω ο κς ανεχωρησεν εις τον ουρνον απο του Ιερεμιου |
v. 14 αγιαστηριον; c adds του θεου | και (2); ab add επαραντες | τα σκευη; ab add
τα αγια | παρεδωκαν; ab add αυτα | γη ab aeth; c adds και τω θυσιαστηριω | καθως
ελαλησεν αυτ. ο κς b aeth de men; c καθως ειπεν κς; a om | ανθωρον c; ab ευθεως | οι
δυο c aeth; ab om | εκλαυσαν; ab add αμα | v. 15 αρον...απελθον ab aeth; c απελθε |
και...λαου; c om | οτι...δοξα ab (aeth); c οτι ευφρασια κυ εις την κεφαλην σου ηξει | v. 16 c
aeth; ab και ταυτα ειπων Ιερεμιας απελυσεν αυτον· Αβιμελεχ δε επορευθη καθα ειπεν αυτω.

IV. 1 την πολιν c aeth; a την πολιν Ιερουσαλημ; b πασαν τ. π. Ιερ.

Εἰσέλθατε εἰς τὴν πόλιν ἡ δύναμις τῶν Χαλδαίων· ἰδοὺ γὰρ
ἠνεῴχθη ὑμῖν ἡ πύλη. Εἰσῆλθεν οὖν ὁ βασιλεὺς μετὰ τοῦ 2
πλήθους αὐτοῦ, καὶ ᾐχμαλώτευσαν πάντα τὸν λαόν. Ἱερεμίας 3
δὲ ἄρας τὰς κλεῖδας τοῦ ναοῦ, ἐξῆλθεν ἔξω τῆς πόλεως, καὶ
ἔρριψεν αὐτὰς ἐνώπιον τοῦ ἡλίου, λέγων· Σοὶ λέγω, ἥλιε, λάβε
τὰς κλεῖδας τοῦ ναοῦ τοῦ Θεοῦ, καὶ φύλαξον αὐτὰς ἕως ἡμέρας,
ἐν ᾗ ἐξετάσει σε Κύριος περὶ αὐτῶν. Διότι ἡμεῖς οὐχ εὑρέθημεν 4
ἄξιοι τοῦ φυλάξαι αὐτάς, ὅτι ἐπίτροποι ψεύδους ἐγενήθημεν.
Ἔτι κλαίοντος Ἱερεμίου τὸν λαόν, εἵλκοντο εἰς Βαβυλῶνα. 5
Ὁ δὲ Βαροὺχ ἐπέθηκε χοῦν ἐπὶ τὴν κεφαλὴν αὐτοῦ, καὶ ἐκάθισε, 6
καὶ ἔκλαυσε τὸν θρῆνον τοῦτον, λέγων· Διὰ τί ἠρημώθη Ἱερουσαλήμ; Διὰ τὰς ἁμαρτίας τοῦ ἠγαπημένου λαοῦ παρεδόθη εἰς
χεῖρας ἐχθρῶν, διὰ τὰς ἁμαρτίας ἡμῶν καὶ τοῦ λαοῦ. Ἀλλὰ 7
μὴ καυχάσθωσαν οἱ παράνομοι, καὶ εἴπωσιν ὅτι, Ἰσχύσαμεν
λαβεῖν τὴν πόλιν τοῦ Θεοῦ ἐν τῇ δυνάμει ἡμῶν. Ἠδυνήθητε ἐπ'
αὐτῇ· ἀλλὰ διὰ τὰς ἁμαρτίας ἡμῶν παρεδόθημεν. Ὁ δὲ Θεὸς 8
ἡμῶν οἰκτειρήσει ἡμᾶς, καὶ ἐπιστρέψει ἡμᾶς εἰς τὴν πόλιν ἡμῶν·
ὑμεῖς δὲ ζωὴν οὐχ ἕξετε. Μακάριοί εἰσιν οἱ πατέρες ἡμῶν, 9
Ἀβραάμ, Ἰσαὰκ καὶ Ἰακώβ, ὅτι ἐξῆλθον ἐκ τοῦ κόσμου τούτου,
καὶ οὐκ εἶδον τὸν ἀφανισμὸν τῆς πόλεως ταύτης. Ταῦτα εἰπών, 10
ἐξῆλθεν, κλαίων καὶ λέγων ὅτι, Λυπούμενος* διὰ σέ, Ἱερουσαλήμ, ἐξῆλθον ἀπὸ σοῦ. Καὶ ἔμεινεν ἐν μνημείῳ καθεζόμενος, 11
τῶν ἀγγέλων ἐρχομένων, καὶ ἐκδιηγουμένων αὐτῷ περὶ πάντων.

V. Ὁ δὲ Ἀβιμέλεχ ἤνεγκε τὰ σῦκα τῷ καύματι, καὶ 1
καταλαβὼν δένδρον, ἐκάθισεν ὑπὸ τὴν σκιὰν αὐτοῦ τοῦ ἀνα-

v. 1 η δυναμις; ab πασα η διν. | πυλη ab; c θυρα | v. 2 εισηλθεν; ab εισελθετω | του πλ.
αυ. ab; c του ιδιου πλ. | ηχμαλωτευσαν; ab αιχμαλωτευσατω | παντα; c om | λαον; c
adds εις Βαβυλωνα | v. 3 κλειδας; c κλεις | εξω...λεγων ab aeth; και ειπεν c | σοι a aeth;
συ bc | λαβε ab; c δεξαι | κλειδας; c κλεις | του θεου; c om (not ab aeth) | εως (v. 3)...
εγενηθημεν (v. 4) with ab aeth; c εως ερωτησιν ποιησει κς περι αυτων εως της συνελευσεως
του ηγαπημενου | end c adds εξενεγκαν ουν αυτον | v. 5 Ιερεμιου; c αυτου | τον λαον; c
om | ειλκοντο; c ειλκοντες | Βαβυλωνα; ab add υπο του βασιλεως των χαλδαιων | v. 6 ὁ
δε Βαρ.; c Ιερεμιας δε διερρηξεν τα ιματια αυτου και | και του λαου ab aeth; c om | v. 7;
c ισχυσαμεν; ηδυνηθημεν ab aeth (?) | τη; c om | ηδυνηθητε επ' αυτη c (aeth); ab om |
παρεδοθημεν ab (?aeth παρεδοθη μεν); c om | v. 8 ημων (1c) ab aeth; c om | οικτειρησει;
c. οικτιρησεν | και επιστρ. ημ. ab aeth; c. om | v. 9 της π. τ. ab aeth; c. ιλημ | v. 10
ειπων; ab add Βαρουχ | εξηλθεν; ab add εξω της πολεως | λυπουμενος; c λοιπου; ab aeth
om | Ιερουσαλημ; c adds και | εξηλθον; c εξηλθε | αποσου; c εκ της πολεως | και λεγ....
σου; aeth om | v. 11 καθεζομενος; c om; aeth? | ερχομενων; ab add προς αυτον, not c
aeth | παντων; ab add ων ο κς εμηνυεν αυτω δι' αυτων.

V. 1 καυματι; aeth adds von dort wohin ihn Jeremias gesandt hatte | καταλαβων;
c κατελαβεν | δενδρον; c adds και | υπο την σκιαν αυτου; c om (not ab aeth) | του ανα-
παηναι bc (b om του); του αναπαυσαι a.

παῆναι ὀλίγον, καὶ κλίνας τὴν κεφαλὴν αὐτοῦ ἐπὶ τὸν κόφινον
τῶν σύκων ὕπνωσεν, κοιμώμενος ἔτη ἑξηκονταέξ· καὶ οὐκ
2 ἐξυπνίσθη ἐκ τοῦ ὕπνου αὐτοῦ. Καὶ μετὰ ταῦτα ἐγερθεὶς
ἀπὸ τοῦ ὕπνου αὐτοῦ, εἶπεν ὅτι, Ἡδέως ἐκοιμήθην ἂν ἄλλο
ὀλίγον, καὶ βεβαρημένη ἐστὶν ἡ κεφαλή μου, ὅτι οὐκ ἐκορέσθην
3 τοῦ ὕπνου μου. Καὶ ἀνακαλύψας τὸν κόφινον τῶν σύκων,
4 εὗρεν αὐτὰ στάζοντα γάλα. Καὶ εἶπεν· Ἤθελον κοιμηθῆναι
5 ὀλίγον, ὅτι βεβαρημένη ἐστὶν ἡ κεφαλή μου· ἀλλὰ φοβοῦμαι,
μήπως κοιμηθῶ καὶ βραδυνῶ τοῦ ἐξυπνισθῆναι, καὶ ὀλιγωρήσῃ
Ἰερεμίας ὁ πατήρ μου· εἰ μὴ γὰρ ἐσπούδαζεν, οὐκ ἂν ἀπέστειλέ
6 με ὄρθρου σήμερον. Ἀναστὰς οὖν πορεύσομαι τῷ καύματι, καὶ
7 *ἀπέλθω ὅπου οὐ καῦμα, οὐ κόπος ἔστιν καθ' ἡμέραν*. Ἐγερθεὶς
οὖν ἦρε τὸν κόφινον τῶν σύκων, καὶ ἐπέθηκεν ἐπὶ τῶν ὤμων
ἑαυτοῦ· καὶ εἰσῆλθεν εἰς Ἰερουσαλὴμ, καὶ οὐκ ἐπέγνω αὐτὴν,
οὔτε τὴν οἰκίαν, οὔτε τὸν τόπον, οὔτε τὸ γένος ἑαυτοῦ, καὶ εἶπεν·
8 Εὐλογητὸς Κύριος, ὅτι μεγάλη ἔκστασις ἐπέπεσεν ἐπ' ἐμέ· οὐκ
9 ἔστιν αὕτη ἡ πόλις· πεπλάνημαι, ὅτι διὰ τῆς ὁδοῦ τοῦ ὄρους
10 ἦλθον, ἐγερθεὶς ἀπὸ τοῦ ὕπνου μου· καὶ βαρείας οὔσης τῆς
κεφαλῆς μου διὰ τὸ μὴ κορεσθῆναί με τοῦ ὕπνου μου, πεπλά-
11 νημαι τὴν ὁδόν. Θαυμαστὸν εἰπεῖν τοῦτο ἐναντίον Ἰερεμίου,
12 ὅτι πεπλάνημαι. Ἐξῆλθε δὲ ἀπὸ τῆς πόλεως· καὶ κατανοήσας
εἶδε τὰ σημεῖα τῆς πόλεως, καὶ εἶπεν· Αὕτη μὲν ἔστιν ἡ πόλις,
13 πεπλάνημαι δέ. Καὶ πάλιν ὑπέστρεψεν εἰς τὴν πόλιν, καὶ
14 ἐζήτησε, καὶ οὐδένα εὗρε τῶν ἰδίων. Καὶ εἶπεν· Εὐλογητὸς
15 Κύριος, ὅτι μεγάλη ἔκστασις ἐπέπεσεν ἐπ' ἐμέ. Καὶ πάλιν

v. 1 κλινας ab; εκλινεν…και c | επιε aeth; υπο ab | των συκων c om (not aeth?) | κοι-
μωμενος ετη εξ. εξ; aeth om; c και εποιησεν εξηκοντα και εξ ετη εκκοιμωμενος | εκ; απο
c | αυτου; ab add κατα προσταξιν θεου δια τον λογον ον ειπεν τω Ιερεμια οτι εγω αυτον
σκεπασω | v. 2 και (1°); c om | εγερθεις; c εξυπνησθεις | ηδεως; b ιδεως | αν αλλο
ολιγον; ab αλλ' ολιγον; c ολιγον; aeth wenn ich doch noch ein wenig schliefe | και
βεβ.; c αλλα βαρια | μου (2°); c aeth om | v. 4 ολιγον; de men αλλο ολιγον | βεβαρη-
μενη; c βαρια | v. 5 ορθρου σημερον c; σημερον ab; beim Lichtwerden aeth | v. 6 text
corrupt; ab ου γαρ καυμα ου κοπος εστιν καθημεραν; c om; aeth denn die Hitze ist ja
heiss und niemals lässt sie ganz und gar nach | v. 7 εγερθεις; αναστας c | των ωμων
ab; την κεφαλην c; aeth om και επεθηκεν…εαυτου | αυτην…εαυτου ab (adding εαυτου
after τοπον); aeth weder die Stadt noch sein Haus; c om ουτε τον τοπον | και ειπεν;
ab ουτε τινα ευρεν κ. ειπ. | v. 8 επ' εμε c adds σημερον (not ab aeth) | ουκ; c και ουκ;
aeth και ελεγεν· ουκ | v. 9 πεπλανημαι; c adds γαρ την οδον | ηλθον; c om | v. 10 πεπλα-
νημαι; ab add δε | v. 11 ειπειν; c εστιν | Ιερεμιου; c του Ι. | οτι πεπλανημαι; c adds
την οδον; aeth wie sich mir die Stadt verandert hat | v. 12 εξηλ. δε; c και εξηλ | κατα-
νοησας ειδε ab; ευρεν c | της πολεως ab; αυτης c | c adds at end την οδον | v. 13 πολιν;
c οδον | και εζητησε; c om | v. 14 και ειπεν; c om | κυριος; ab ο κυριος; ει κυριε c | εμε;
c adds και ουκ εστιν αυτη η πολις | v. 15 παλιν; c om (not ab aeth).

ἐξῆλθεν ἔξω τῆς πόλεως. Καὶ ἔμεινε λυπούμενος, μὴ εἰδὼς
ποῦ ἀπέλθῃ. Καὶ ἀπέθηκε τὸν κόφινον, λέγων· Καθέζομαι 16
ὧδε, ἕως ὁ Κύριος ἄρῃ τὴν ἔκστασιν ταύτην ἀπ' ἐμοῦ. Καθη- 17
μένου δὲ αὐτοῦ, εἰδέ τινα γηραιὸν ἐρχόμενον ἐξ ἀγροῦ, καὶ λέγει
αὐτῷ Ἀβιμέλεχ· Σοὶ λέγω, πρεσβῦτα, ποία ἐστὶν ἡ πόλις
αὕτη; Καὶ εἶπεν αὐτῷ· Ἱερουσαλήμ ἐστι. Καὶ λέγει αὐτῷ 18
Ἀβιμέλεχ· Ποῦ ἔστιν ὁ Ἱερεμίας ὁ ἱερεύς, καὶ Βαρούχ ὁ
ἀναγνώστης, καὶ πᾶς ὁ λαὸς τῆς πόλεως ταύτης, ὅτι οὐχ
εὗρον αὐτούς; Καὶ εἶπεν αὐτῷ ὁ πρεσβύτης· Οὐκ εἶ σὺ 19
ἐκ τῆς πόλεως ταύτης, σήμερον μνησθεὶς τοῦ Ἱερεμίου, ὅτι 20
ἐπερωτᾷς περὶ αὐτοῦ μετὰ τοσοῦτον χρόνον; Ἱερεμίας γὰρ 21
ἐν Βαβυλῶνί ἐστι μετὰ τοῦ λαοῦ· ᾐχμαλωτεύθησαν γὰρ ὑπὸ
Ναβουχοδονόσορ τοῦ βασιλέως, καὶ μετ' αὐτῶν ἐστιν Ἱερεμίας
εὐαγγελίσασθαι αὐτοῖς καὶ κατηχῆσαι αὐτοὺς τὸν λόγον. Εὐθὺς 22
δὲ ἀκούσας Ἀβιμέλεχ παρὰ τοῦ γηραιοῦ ἀνθρώπου, εἶπεν· Εἰ 23
μὴ ἦς πρεσβύτης, καὶ ὅτι οὐκ ἐξὸν ἀνθρώπῳ ὑβρίσαι τὸν
μείζονα αὐτοῦ, ἐπικατεγέλων ἄν σοι καὶ ἔλεγον, ὅτι μαίνῃ·
ὅτι εἶπας, ᾘχμαλωτεύθη ὁ λαὸς εἰς Βαβυλῶνα. Εἰ ἦσαν 24
οἱ καταρράκται τοῦ οὐρανοῦ κατελθόντες ἐπ' αὐτούς; οὔπω
ἐστὶ καιρὸς ἀπελθεῖν εἰς Βαβυλῶνα. Πόση γὰρ ὥρα ἐστίν, 25
ἀφ' οὗ ἀπέστειλέ με ὁ πατήρ μου Ἱερεμίας εἰς τὸ χωρίον τοῦ
Ἀγρίππα ἐπὶ ὀλίγα σῦκα, ἵνα δίδωμεν τοῖς νοσοῦσι τοῦ
λαοῦ, καὶ ἀπελθὼν ἤνεγκον αὐτά, καὶ ἐλθὼν ἐπί τι δένδρον 26
τῷ καύματι, ἐκάθισα τοῦ ἀναπαῆναι ὀλίγον, καὶ ἔκλινα τὴν
κεφαλήν μου ἐπὶ τὸν κόφινον, καὶ ἐκοιμήθην, καὶ ἐξυπνισθεὶς

ν. 15 πολεως; ab add και ελεγεν· τα μεν σημεια της πολεως εισιν (sic) | ειδως; c ιδων |
απελθη c; απελθειν ab | και απεθηκεν ab aeth; αφηκεν δε c | κοφινον; c adds των συκων;
aeth? | v. 16 εως; c adds αν | v. 17 καθημενου; καθεζομενος c | γηραιον; c γηραον αυον |
ερχ.; c om | λεγει; c ειπεν | Αβιμελεχ ab aeth; c om | σοι; b συ | πρεσβυτα; abc men
πρεσβυτα | αυτω; c om | Ιερουσαλημ; aeth das alte Jerusalem | v. 18 λεγει; c ειπεν |
που; ab και που | εστιν; ab εισιν | ιερευς aeth; ab ιερευς του θεου; c αρχιερευς | ο ανα-
γνωστης; c om; aeth der Levit | v. 19 αυτω ο πρ. c aeth; ο πρ. τω Αβιμελεχ ab | v. 20
μνησθεις; c εμνησθης | μετα τοσ. χρ.; aeth. obgleich du diese ganze Zeit da sassest |
v. 21 υπο; c υπο του | βασιλεως; c adds Βαβυλωνος; aeth von Persien | εστιν Ιερ.; c
απηλθεν | και κατ. αυτους ab (αυτοις b); a aeth om | τον λογον abc; aeth om | v. 23 οτι;
c om | ανθρωπω (aeth); ab ανθρωπω θεου; c ανθρωπων | επικατεγελων αν; κατ. αν de
men; επει καταγελων ab; επικατεγελουν c | σοι c; σου bde men; a om | και ελεγον; a
om | μαινη a aeth; μενει b; μεν c | οτι ειπας; c om | ηχμαλ.; c ηχμαλωτευσον | v. 24
ουπω; c ουπω ουκ | καιρος; c om | απελθειν; c πορευθηναι | v. 25 αφ' ου; c εξοτου | εις
...Αγριππα; c om (not aeth ab) | επι; c ενεγκαι | συκα; ab add ενεγκαι; c aeth om |
ινα διδ...λαου; c τοις νοσουσιν | v. 26 απελθων; c om | ηνεγκον αυτα και ελθων; ab om;
aeth ich bin gegangen und dorthin gelangt und habe genommen was er mir befohlen
hat und habe mich umgewandt, und indem ich ging | τι; c om | εκαθισα...κοφινον (1°);
c om | εκοιμηθην; ab add ολιγον | εξυπνισθεις; c αναστας.

ἀπεκάλυψα τὸν κόφινον τῶν σύκων, νομίζων ὅτι ἐβράδυνα, καὶ
εὗρον τὰ σῦκα στάζοντα γάλα, καθὼς συνέλεξα αὐτά. Σὺ δὲ
27 λέγεις, ὅτι ἠχμαλωτεύθη ὁ λαὸς εἰς Βαβυλῶνα; Ἵνα δὲ γνῷς,
28 λάβε, ἴδε τὰ σῦκα. Καὶ ἀνεκάλυψε τὸν κόφινον τῶν σύκων
29 τῷ γέροντι. Καὶ εἶδεν αὐτὰ στάζοντα γάλα. Ἰδὼν δὲ αὐτὰ
30 ὁ γηραιὸς ἄνθρωπος, εἶπεν· Ὦ υἱέ μου, δίκαιος ἄνθρωπος εἶ σύ,
καὶ οὐκ ἠθέλησεν ὁ Θεὸς δεῖξαί σοι τὴν ἐρήμωσιν τῆς πόλεως.
Ἤνεγκε γὰρ ταύτην τὴν ἔκστασιν ἐπὶ σὲ ὁ Θεός. Ἰδοὺ γὰρ
ἐξήκοντα καὶ ἓξ ἔτη σήμερόν εἰσιν ἀφ' οὗ ἠχμαλωτεύθη ὁ λαὸς
31 εἰς Βαβυλῶνα. Καὶ ἵνα μάθῃς, τέκνον, ὅτι ἀληθές ἐστιν, ἀνά-
βλεψον εἰς τὸν ἀγρὸν καὶ ἴδε, ὅτι ἐφάνη ἡ αὔξησις τῶν γενημά-
των· ἴδε καὶ τὰ σῦκα, ὅτι καιρὸς αὐτῶν οὐκ ἔστι, καὶ γνῶθι.
32 Τότε ἔκραξε μεγάλῃ φωνῇ Ἀβιμέλεχ, λέγων· Εὐλογήσω σε,
Κύριε ὁ Θεὸς τοῦ οὐρανοῦ καὶ τῆς γῆς, ἡ ἀνάπαυσις τῶν ψυχῶν
33 τῶν δικαίων ἐν παντὶ τόπῳ. Καὶ λέγει τῷ γηραιῷ ἀνθρώπῳ·
Ποῖός ἐστιν ὁ μὴν οὗτος; Ὁ δὲ εἶπε· Νισσάν· *καὶ ἔστιν ἡ
34 δωδεκάτη*. Καὶ ἐπάρας ἐκ τῶν σύκων, ἔδωκε τῷ γηραιῷ ἀνθρώπῳ, καὶ λέγει αὐτῷ· Ὁ Θεὸς φωταγωγήσει σε εἰς τὴ ἄνω
πόλιν Ἰερουσαλήμ.
1 VI. Μετὰ ταῦτα ἐξῆλθεν Ἀβιμέλεχ ἔξω τῆς πόλεως, καὶ
προσηύξατο πρὸς Κύριον. Καὶ ἰδοὺ ἄγγελος Κυρίου ἦλθε,
καὶ ἀπεκατέστησεν αὐτόν, ὅπου ἦν Βαρούχ· εὗρε δὲ αὐτὸν ἐν
2 μνημείῳ καθεζόμενον. Καὶ ἐν τῷ θεωρῆσαι ἀλλήλους, ἔκλαυσαν

v. 26 απεκαλυψα; c ανεκαλυψα | εβραδυνα; c εχρονησα | τα συκα; c αυτα; (aeth?) |
συνελεξα; c ανελεξαμην | ηχμ. ὁ λαος; c ηχμαλωτευθησαν | v. 30 δικαιος...συ c (aeth); ab
δικαιου ανου υιος ει συ | δειξαι σοι c aeth; ab ιδειν σε | πολεως; ab add ταυτης; not c aeth |
γαρ (1°); c om | ο θεος; c om | σημερον εισιν c (aeth); ab om | ηχμ. ὁ λαος; c αιχμα-
λωτευθησαν | v. 31 τεκνον; c om | αληθες εστιν; ab αληθη εισιν απερ λεγω σοι | οτι...
γνωθι aeth, ab (οτι ουκ) (α γεννηματων); c οτι ουκ εστι καιρος των συκων | fin aeth adds
und er erkannte dass die Zeit von alle diesen nicht war | v. 32 τοτε; c και | Αβιμελεχ;
c om | ευλογησω; c ευλογω | κυριε ο θεος; ab ο θεος; c κυριε; aeth O Herr mein Gott,
Gott | των ψυχων; c om | τοπω ab aeth; c καιρω | r. 33 και λεγει τω γηραιω ανω; c το
φως το αληθινον· η αληθινη ανταποδοσις, ο ων μεγας, θαυμαστος εις τους αιωνας αμην.
τοτε λεγει τω γη. αν. | Νισσαν και ε. δωδ. ; ab Νισσαν· ο εστι δωδεκατος; c Ισαακ εστιν
ο μην ουτος; aeth der zwölfte des Monats Nisan welcher Mijazja ist. The Ethiopic
text must be right: for Nisan is not the twelfth month, either in civil or ecclе-
siastical reckoning. A reference to Ezra viii. 15 will shew the passage on which
our writer works: "we departed from the river of Ahava on the twelfth day of
the first month to go unto Jerusalem": the 12th of Nisan is here meant, the return
commencing in Nisan, in order that Jerusalem may be reached in Ab: cf. Ezra pas-
sim. Or can it be Νισσαν ο εστιν Αβιβ? v. 34 και επαρας; c ουτος αρας ουν | και
λεγει; c ειπων | εις; ab επι.
VI. 1 προσηυξατο; c ηυξατο | ηλθε και; ab add κρατησας αυτου της δεξιας χειρος |
αυτον; ab add εις τον τοπον | Βαρουχ; ab add καθεζομενος | ευρε δε; c και ευρε | καθε-
ζομενον; ab om | v. 2 εκλ. αμφ. b (aeth); a om; c εκλαυσαν.

ἀμφότεροι καὶ κατεφίλησαν ἀλλήλους. Ἀναβλέψας δὲ Βαροὺχ,
εἶδε τὰ σῦκα ἐσκεπασμένα ἐν τῷ κοφίνῳ· καὶ ἄρας τοὺς
ὀφθαλμοὺς αὐτοῦ εἰς τὸν οὐρανὸν, προσηύξατο λέγων· Ἔστι
Θεὸς ὁ παρέχων μισθαποδοσίαν τοῖς ἁγίοις αὐτοῦ. Ἑτοίμασον 3
σεαυτὴν, ἡ καρδία μου, καὶ εὐφραίνου, καὶ ἀγάλλου ἐν τῷ
2 Cor. v. 1. σκηνώματί σου, λέγω τῷ σαρκικῷ οἴκῳ σου· τὸ πένθος σου
γὰρ μετεστράφη εἰς χαράν. Ἔρχεται γὰρ ὁ ἱκανὸς, καὶ ἀρεῖ
σε ἐκ τοῦ σκηνώματός σου. Οὐ γὰρ γέγονέ σοι ἁμαρτία.
Ἀνάψυξον ἡ παρθενική μου πίστις, καὶ πίστευσον ὅτι ζήσεις. 4
Ἐπίβλεψον ἐπὶ τὸν κόφινον τοῦτον τῶν σύκων· ἰδοὺ γὰρ ἑξη- 5
κονταὲξ ἔτη ἐποίησαν, καὶ οὐκ ἐμαράνθησαν, οὐδὲ ὤζεσαν, ἀλλὰ
στάζουσι τοῦ γάλακτος. Οὕτως γίνεταί σοι ἡ σάρξ μου, ἐὰν 6
ποιήσῃς τὰ προσταχθέντα σου ὑπὸ τοῦ ἀγγέλου τῆς δικαιοσύνης. Ὁ φυλάξας τὸν κόφινον τῶν σύκων, αὐτὸς πάλιν 7
φυλάξει σε ἐν τῇ δυνάμει αὐτοῦ. Ταῦτα εἰπὼν ὁ Βαροὺχ, 8
λέγει τῷ Ἀβιμέλεχ· Ἀνάστηθι, καὶ εὐξώμεθα, ἵνα γνωρίσῃ
ἡμῖν ὁ Κύριος τὸ, πῶς δυνησώμεθα ἀποστεῖλαι τὴν φάσιν τῷ
Ἱερεμίᾳ εἰς Βαβυλῶνα διὰ τὴν γενομένην σοι σκέπην. Καὶ 9
ηὔξατο Βαροὺχ, λέγων· Ἡ δύναμις ἡμῶν, ὁ Θεὸς ἡμῶν Κύριε,
τὸ ἐκλεκτὸν φῶς, τὸ ἐξελθὸν ἐκ στόματος αὐτοῦ, παρακαλῶ
καὶ δέομαί σου τῆς ἀγαθότητος· τὸ μέγα ὄνομα, ὃ οὐδεὶς δύναται
γνῶναι· ἄκουσον τῆς φωνῆς τοῦ δούλου σου, καὶ γενοῦ γνῶσις 10
ἐν τῇ καρδίᾳ μου. Τί θέλεις ποιήσωμεν; πῶς ἀποστείλω πρὸς

v. 2 αλληλους (2°); b repeats εν τω θεωρ. αλλ. | αναβλεψας; aeth om | δε; ab om | Βα-
ρουχ; ab add τοις οφθαλμοις αυτου (b τους οφθ. α.) | κοφινω; ab add του Αβιμελεχ (not
c aeth) | αρας ab; c (aeth) επηρεν | προσηυξατο λεγων ab (aeth); c ειπεν | εστιν ab; εις
εστιν o c; gross ist Gott aeth | αγιοις αυτου c (aeth seinen Gerechten); ab τοις αγαπωσι
σε | v. 3 η; c om | αγαλλου ab; c αγαλλιασον | εν; c aeth λεγων | λεγω; c aeth om | οικω
σου; c τω οικω σου αγιω | μετεστραφη; c μεταστραφητω· aeth μεταστραφησεται | γαρ
(2°); c om | αρει; c ερει | εκ τ. σκη; c. εν τω σκηνωματι; aeth und wird dich in deinen
Körper zurückkehren lassen | γεγονε; c εγενετο εν; aeth omits clause | v. 4 ab
αναψυξον εν τω σκηνωματι σου, εν τη παρθενικη σου ποιμνη; c αναστηθι αναστρεψον
εις το ιδιον σου η παρθενικη μου πιστις; aeth schaue auf deine Jungfräulichkeit des
Glaubens | οτι; c και | v. 5 τουτον ab (aeth); c om | v. 6 προσταχθεντα σου ab (aeth
deinen Befehl); c προσετεταχθεντα (!) σοι | v. 8 λεγει τω Αβ.; c ειπεν ο Αβ.; cf aeth,
antwortete Abimelech und sagte zu ihm | το; c om | δυνησωμεθα ab; c δυναμεθα | φα-
σιν; c adds ταυτην (not aeth) | δια...σκεπην; ab δια την σκεπην την γενομενην σοι εν τη
οδω; c δια την σκεπην σου; aeth die Beschützung mit der du mich bedeckt hast | v. 9
Βαρουχ; ab add και Αβιμελεχ | λεγων; ab λεγοντες | η δυναμις ημων ο θς ημων κε ab;
o θς κς η δυναμις μου c aeth (meine Kraft ist Gott, der Herr) | εκλεκτον; aeth om |
εκ; c εκ του | παρακαλω και δεομαι c aeth; ab παρακαλουμεν και δεομεθα | της αγ.; c
την αγαθοτητα | ονομα; ab add σου | γνωναι; c add αυτω | v. 10 του δουλου c aeth;
ab των δουλων | μου c aeth; ab ημων | τι θε. ποιησ.; ab τι ποιησωμεν; c εως αν το (sic)
θελω ποιησω; aeth (?) | πως αποστ.; ab πως αποστειλωμεν; c εως αν αποστειλω; aeth
und ich schicke.

11 Ἱερεμίαν εἰς Βαβυλῶνα ; Ἔτι δὲ προσευχομένου τοῦ Βαρούχ,
12 ἰδοὺ ἄγγελος Κυρίου ἦλθε, καὶ λέγει τῷ Βαρούχ· Βαρούχ, ὁ
σύμβουλος τοῦ φωτός, Μὴ μεριμνήσῃς τὸ, πῶς ἀποστείλῃς πρὸς Ἱερεμίαν· ἔρχεται γὰρ πρός σε ὥρα τοῦ φωτὸς
13 αὔριον ἀετὸς, καὶ σὺ ἐπισκέψῃ πρὸς Ἱερεμίαν. Γράψον οὖν
ἐν τῇ ἐπιστολῇ ὅτι, Λάλησον τοῖς υἱοῖς Ἰσραήλ· Ὁ γενόμενος
ἐν ὑμῖν ξένος, ἀφορισθήτω, καὶ ποιήσωσι ιέ ἡμέρας· καὶ μετὰ
14 ταῦτα εἰσάξω ὑμᾶς εἰς τὴν πόλιν ὑμῶν, λέγει Κύριος. Ὁ μὴ
ἀφοριζόμενος ἐκ τῆς Βαβυλῶνος, ὦ Ἱερεμία, οὐ μὴ εἰσέλθῃ εἰς τὴν
πόλιν· καὶ ἐπιτιμῶ αὐτοῖς, τοῦ μὴ ἀποδεχθῆναι αὐτοὺς αὖθις ὑπὸ
15 τῶν Βαβυλωνιτῶν, λέγει Κύριος. ·Καὶ ταῦτα εἰπὼν ὁ ἄγγελος,
16 ἀπῆλθεν ἀπὸ τοῦ Βαρούχ. Ὁ δὲ Βαρούχ ἀποστείλας εἰς τὴν
ἀγορὰν τῶν ἐθνῶν, ἤνεγκε χάρτην καὶ μέλανα, καὶ ἔγραψεν
17 ἐπιστολὴν περιέχουσαν οὕτως· Βαρούχ ὁ δοῦλος τοῦ Θεοῦ γράφει
τῷ Ἱερεμίᾳ· Ὁ ἐν τῇ αἰχμαλωσίᾳ τῆς Βαβυλῶνος, χαῖρε καὶ
ἀγαλλιῶ, ὅτι ὁ Θεὸς οὐκ ἀφῆκεν ἡμᾶς ἐξελθεῖν ἐκ τοῦ σώματος
τούτου λυπουμένους διὰ τὴν πόλιν τὴν ἐρημωθεῖσαν καὶ ὑβρι-
18 σθεῖσαν. Διὰ τοῦτο ἐσπλαγχνίσθη ὁ Κύριος ἐπὶ τῶν δακρύων
ἡμῶν, καὶ ἐμνήσθη τῆς διαθήκης, ἧς ἔστησε μετὰ τῶν πατέρων
19 ἡμῶν Ἀβραὰμ, καὶ Ἰσαὰκ, καὶ Ἰακώβ. Ἀπέστειλε γὰρ πρός
με τὸν ἄγγελον αὐτοῦ, καὶ εἶπέ μοι τοὺς λόγους τούτους, οὓς
20 ἀπέστειλα πρός σε. Οὗτοι οὖν εἰσιν οἱ λόγοι, οὓς εἶπε Κύριος
ὁ Θεὸς Ἰσραὴλ, ὁ ἐξαγαγὼν ἡμᾶς ἐκ γῆς Αἰγύπτου, ἐκ τῆς
21 μεγάλης καμίνου· Ὅτι οὐκ ἐφυλάξατε τὰ δικαιώματά μου,
ἀλλὰ ὑψώθη ἡ καρδία ὑμῶν, καὶ ἐτραχηλιάσατε ἐνώπιόν μου,
ἐθυμώθην καὶ ἐν ὀργῇ παρέδωκα ὑμᾶς τῇ καμίνῳ εἰς Βαβυλῶνα.
22 Ἐὰν οὖν ἀκούσητε τῆς φωνῆς μου, λέγει Κύριος, ἐκ στόματος
Ἱερεμίου τοῦ παιδός μου, ὁ ἀκούων, ἀναφέρω αὐτὸν ἐκ τῆς Βαβυλῶνος, ὁ δὲ μὴ ἀκούων, ξένος γενήσεται τῆς Ἱερουσαλὴμ καὶ

v. 10 Βαβυλωνα; ab add την φασιν ταιτην | v. 11 Βαρουχ (1°); ab add και του Αβι-
μελεχ | ηλθε; c om | λεγει; c ειπεν | Βαρουχ; ab add απαντας τους λογους τουτους |
v. 12 Βαρουχ c aeth; ab om | φωτος; ab add λεγει | μεριμνησης c aeth; ab μεριμνη-
σητε | αποστειλης c aeth; ab αποστειλητε | γαρ; c om | προς; c τον | v. 13 λαλησον; c
ειπατε | ο; c οτι | ξενος; c εξ ενος | v. 14 ω Ιερ.; ab om | επιτιμω a; bc επετιμων | αυ-
τους c; ab om | υπο; ab om | v. 15 και; c om | απηλθεν; c ανεχωρησεν | v. 16 ab
αποστειλας δε εις την διασποραν των εθνων ηνεγκεν χαρτην και μελανα και εγραψεν
επιστολην περιεχουσαν ουτως; c ο δε Βαρουχ απεστειλεν εις την αγωραν των εθνων και
ηνεγκεν χαρτην και μελαν και εγρ. επ. λεγων οτι; aeth und Baruch geleitete ihn bis zur
Strasse und holte Papier und Tinte und schrieb folgendermassen | v. 17 ο (2°); c om;
aeth τω | αγαλλιω a; αγαλλιου b; αγαλλιασον c | v. 19 απεστειλα ab aeth; αποστελλω
c | v. 20 εκ (2°); c om | v. 21 εθυμωθην c; om ab aeth | εν οργη και θυμω ab; c aeth
om | v. 22 ουν; c om | αναφερω c (aeth); αφορισω ab | της Βαβ.; του λακκου της Βαβ.
c | γενησεται; a γενηται; c γινεται | και της Βαβ.; ab om; aeth und sie werden nicht

τῆς Βαβυλῶνος. Δοκιμάσεις δὲ αὐτοὺς ἐκ τοῦ ὕδατος τοῦ 23
Ἰορδάνου· ὁ μὴ ἀκούων φανερὸς γενήσεται· τοῦτο τὸ σημεῖόν
ἐστι τῆς μεγάλης σφραγῖδος. VII. Καὶ ἀνέστη Βαροὺχ, καὶ ἐξῆλθεν ἐκ τοῦ μνημείου. 1
Καὶ ἀποκριθεὶς ἀνθρωπίνῃ φωνῇ ὁ ἀετὸς, εἶπε· Χαῖρε, Βαρούχ, 2
ὁ οἰκονόμος τῆς πίστεως. Καὶ εἶπεν αὐτῷ Βαρούχ ὅτι, Ἐκλεκ- 3
τός εἶ σὺ ὁ λαλῶν, ἐκ πάντων τῶν πετεινῶν τοῦ οὐρανοῦ· ἐκ
τῆς γὰρ αὐγῆς τῶν ὀφθαλμῶν δῆλόν ἐστι. Δεῖξόν μοι οὖν, τί 4
ποιεῖς ἐνταῦθα; Καὶ εἶπεν αὐτῷ ὁ ἀετός· Ἀπεστάλην ὧδε, ὅπως 5
πᾶσαν φάσιν ἣν θέλεις, ἀποστείλῃς δι᾽ ἐμοῦ. Καὶ εἶπεν αὐτῷ 6
Βαρούχ· Εἰ δύνασαι σὺ ἐπᾶραι τὴν φάσιν ταύτην τῷ Ἰερεμίᾳ
εἰς Βαβυλῶνα; Καὶ εἶπεν αὐτῷ ὁ ἀετός· Εἰς τοῦτο γὰρ καὶ 7
ἀπεστάλην. Καὶ ἄρας Βαροὺχ τὴν ἐπιστολὴν, καὶ δεκαπέντε 8
σῦκα ἐκ τοῦ κοφίνου τοῦ Ἀβιμέλεχ, ἔδησεν εἰς τὸν τράχηλον
τοῦ ἀετοῦ, καὶ εἶπεν αὐτῷ· Σοὶ λέγω, βασιλεῦ τῶν πετεινῶν, 9
ἄπελθε ἐν εἰρήνῃ μεθ᾽ ὑγείας, καὶ τὴν φάσιν ἔνεγκόν μοι. Μὴ 10
ὁμοιωθῇς τῷ κόρακι, ὃν ἐξαπέστειλε Νῶε, καὶ οὐκ ἀπεστράφη
ἔτι πρὸς αὐτὸν εἰς τὴν κιβωτόν· ἀλλὰ ὁμοιώθητι τῇ περιστερᾷ,
ἥτις ἐκ τρίτου φάσιν ἤνεγκε τῷ δικαίῳ· οὕτω καὶ σὺ, ἆρον τὴν 11
καλὴν φάσιν ταύτην τῷ Ἰερεμίᾳ καὶ τοῖς σὺν αὐτῷ, ἵνα εὖ σοι
γένηται, ἆρον τὸν χάρτην τοῦτον τῷ λαῷ τῷ ἐκλεκτῷ τοῦ Θεοῦ.
Ἐὰν κυκλώσωσί σε πάντα τὰ πετεινὰ τοῦ οὐρανοῦ, καὶ πάντες 12
οἱ ἐχθροὶ τῆς ἀληθείας βουλόμενοι πολεμῆσαι μετὰ σοῦ, ἀγώνι-
σαι· ὁ Κύριος δώῃ σοι δύναμιν. Καὶ μὴ ἐκκλίνῃς εἰς τὰ δεξιὰ,
μήτε εἰς τὰ ἀριστερά, ἀλλ᾽ ὡς βέλος ὕπαγον ὀρθῶς, οὕτως ἄπελθε
ἐν τῇ δυνάμει τοῦ Θεοῦ. Τότε ὁ ἀετὸς ἐπετάσθη, ἔχων τὴν 13

---

verbannt von Jerusalem in Babylon sein.

v. 23 δοκιμασω a; δοκημασει b; δοκιμασης c (aeth) | γενησεται; c γινεται | το; ab om.

VII. 2 Text with ab aeth; c και ευρεν τον αετον καθεζομενον εκτος του μνημιου
και ειπεν αυτω ο αετος | πιστεως ab aeth; πολεως c | r. 3 αυτω; c om | συ ο; c
om | r. 4 ουν; c om | ειπεν αυτω; ab om αυτω | v. 5 απ. ab aeth; c ο θς απεστειλεν
με | ωδε; ab add προς σε | πα. φα. ; c προς πα. φα. | δι᾽ εμου; c με | v. 6 ειπεν;
c λεγει | δυνασαι συ a; δυνη συ b; δυνηση c | επαραι; c αραι | ειπεν; c λεγει | r. 7 εις;
εγω εις ab | γαρ και; ab om | r. 8 αυτω; c om | v. 9 βασιλευ; c ο βασιλευς | πετεινων;
c ορνεων | ενεγκον c; ενεγκαι ab | v. 10 ετι προς αυτον; ab om (not c aeth) | v. 11 τοις συν
αυτω; c τοις δεσμιοις αυτου; aeth. die welcher von Israel bei ihm sind | τον χαρτην
τουτον; sic ab; c aeth ταυτην την χαραν (aeth diese Freudenbotschaft) | εκλεκτω;
c και τω εκλεκτω | r. 12 κυκλωσωσι; ab κυκλωσουσι | παντες...αληθειας c aeth; ab
om | βουλομενοι; ab βουλωνται | δωη ab aeth; δωση c | εις τα δεξια ac; δεξια b | μητε εις
τα; ab η | υπαγον ορθως; a υπαγων ορ.; c υπαγων | ουτως; c aeth om | απελθε; c
υπαγε | end of verse; ab add και εσται η δοξα κυ εν παση τη οδω η πορευση (not
c aeth).

ἐπιστολὴν, καὶ ἀπῆλθεν εἰς Βαβυλῶνα, καὶ ἀνεπαύσατο ἐπί τι
ξύλον ἔξω τῆς πόλεως εἰς τόπον ἔρημον· ἐσιώπησε δὲ ἕως οὗ
14 διῆλθεν Ἰερεμίας, αὐτὸς καὶ ἄλλοι τινὲς τοῦ λαοῦ· ἐξήρχοντο
γὰρ θάψαι νεκρόν· καὶ γὰρ ᾐτήσατο Ἰερεμίας παρὰ τοῦ Ναβουχοδονόσορ, λέγων· Δός μοι τόπον, ποῦ θάψω τοὺς νεκροὺς τοῦ
15 λαοῦ μου. Καὶ ἔδωκεν αὐτῷ. Ἀπερχομένων δὲ αὐτῶν καὶ
κλαιόντων μετὰ τοῦ νεκροῦ, ἦλθον κατέναντι τοῦ ἀετοῦ· καὶ
ἔκραξεν ὁ ἀετός, λέγων· Σοὶ λέγω, Ἰερεμία ὁ ἐκλεκτὸς τοῦ Θεοῦ,
ἄπελθε, σύναξον τὸν λαὸν ἅπαντα, καὶ ἔλθωσιν ὧδε, ἵνα ἀκού-
σωσι τοῦ καλοῦ κηρύγματος, ὃ ἤνεγκά σοι ἀπὸ τοῦ Βαρούχ καὶ
16 τοῦ Ἀβιμέλεχ. Ἀκούσας δὲ ὁ Ἰερεμίας, ἐδόξασε τὸν Θεόν·
καὶ ἀπελθὼν συνῆξε τὸν λαὸν σὺν γυναιξὶ καὶ τέκνοις, καὶ
17 ἦλθεν ὅπου ὁ ἀετός. Καὶ κατῆλθεν ὁ ἀετὸς ἐπὶ τὸν τεθνηκότα,
18 καὶ ἀνέζησε· γέγονε δὲ τοῦτο, ἵνα πιστεύσωσιν. Ἐθαύμασε δὲ
πᾶς ὁ λαὸς ἐπὶ τῷ γεγονότι, λέγοντες ὅτι, Μὴ οὗτος ἔστι ὁ Θεὸς
ὁ ὀφθεὶς τοῖς πατράσιν ἡμῶν ἐν τῇ ἐρήμῳ διὰ Μωϋσέως, καὶ
ἐποίησεν ἑαυτὸν ἐν σχήματι ἀετοῦ καὶ ἐφάνη ἡμῖν διὰ τοῦ
19 μεγάλου ἀετοῦ τούτου; Καὶ εἶπεν ὁ ἀετὸς τῷ Ἰερεμίᾳ, Δεῦρο
λῦσον τὴν ἐπιστολὴν ταύτην, καὶ ἀνάγνωθι αὐτὴν τῷ λαῷ.
20 Λύσας οὖν τὴν ἐπιστολὴν, ἀνέγνω τῷ λαῷ. Ἀκούσας οὖν ὁ λαὸς,
ἔκλαυσαν, καὶ ἐπέθηκαν χοῦν ἐπὶ τὴν κεφαλὴν αὐτῶν· καὶ ἔλε-
21 γον τῷ Ἰερεμίᾳ· Σῶσον ἡμᾶς καὶ ἀπάγγειλον ἡμῖν, τί ποιήσω-
22 μεν, ἵνα εἰσέλθωμεν πάλιν εἰς τὴν πόλιν ἡμῶν; Ἀποκριθεὶς δὲ
Ἰερεμίας εἶπεν αὐτοῖς· Πάντα ὅσα ἐκ τῆς ἐπιστολῆς ἠκούσατε,

v. 13 επιστολην ; c adds εν τω τραχηλω αυτου | ανεπαυσατο c aeth ; ελθων ανε-
παυσατο ab | τι ξυλον ab ; c στυλον ; aeth auf einer Saüle and explains the τόπος
ἔρημος as eine Stelle des unbekannten Landes | ου διηλθεν ; c αν παρελθη | αυτος κτέ ;
ab αυτος γαρ και ο λαος εξηρχοντο ; c αυτος γαρ και αλλοι τινες του λαου· απηρχοντο
γαρ | v. 14 νεκρον ; ab add εξω της πολεως | και γαρ ητ. ; c ητ. γαρ | του Ναβουχ.; ab
του βασιλεως Ναβ. (not c aeth) | που c aeth ; ab οπως | αυτω ; ab add ο βασιλευς |
v. 15 κατεναντι ; c εναντιον | σοι λεγω ab aeth ; c om | απαντα c aeth ; ab om !
ελθωσιν ωδε ; ab ιλθε ενταυθα ; aeth (?) es soll hieher kommen | του κ. κηρ. ο ην.
aeth ; c τ. κ. κη. του θυ ο ην.; ab επιστολης ης ηνεγκα | του Βαρ. και του Αβ.; c Βαρ.
και Αβ. | v. 17 και κατηλθεν ο αετος ; c om (ὅμοιοτ.) | ανεζησε ; ab add και ανεστη | γεγονε
δε τουτο ab ; τουτο δε εγενετο c ; aeth und dieses that er | v. 18 μη...Θς c ; ab εστιν θς ;
aeth vielleicht ist dies der Gott' και εποιησεν...τουτου c (aeth) ; ab και νυν εφανη
ημιν δια του αετου τουτου | v. 19 τω Ιερ.; ab σοι λεγω Ιερ. | αυτην τω λαω c aeth ; ab εις
τα ωτα του λαου | ανεγνω ; c adds αυτην (not aeth) | v. 20 ακουσας ουν c (? aeth) ;
ab ακουσαντες δε πας | εκλαυσαν ab aeth ; εκλαυσεν c | επεθηκαν ab aeth ; επεθηκεν
c | την κεφαλ. αυτων aeth ; ab τας κεφαλας αυτων ; c την κεφαλην αυτου | v. 21 σωσον
ημας και c aeth (rette uns!) ; ab om | ινα ; c πως | παλιν ; c om | v. 22 αποκρ. δε Ιερ.
ειπεν αυτοις c ; ab και ειπεν προς αυτους ; aeth und Jeremias erhob sich und sagte zu
ihnen | εκ της επιστολης ; ab om (not c aeth) | ηκουσατε ; c om.

φυλάξατε· καὶ εἰσάξει ἡμᾶς εἰς τὴν πόλιν ἡμῶν. Ἔγραψε δὲ καὶ 23
ἐπιστολὴν ὁ Ἱερεμίας πρὸς Βαροὺχ, οὕτως λέγων· Υἱέ μου ἀγα-
πητέ, μὴ ἀμελήσῃς ἐν ταῖς προσευχαῖς σου δεόμενος ὑπὲρ ἡμῶν
ὅπως κατευοδεύσῃ τὴν ὁδὸν ἡμῶν, ἄχρις ἂν ἐξέλθωμεν ἐκ τῶν
προσταγμάτων τοῦ ἀνόμου βασιλέως τούτου· δίκαιος γὰρ εὑρέ-
θης ἐνάντιον αὐτοῦ καὶ οὐκ ἔασέν σε εἰσελθεῖν ἐνταῦθα μεθ'
ἡμῶν, ὅπως μὴ ἴδῃς τὴν κάκωσιν τὴν γενομένην τῷ λαῷ ὑπὸ τῶν
Βαβυλωνίων· ὥσπερ γὰρ πατὴρ, υἱὸν μονογενῆ ἔχων, τούτου δὲ 24
παραδοθέντος εἰς τιμωρίαν· οἱ οὖν ἰδόντες τὸν πατέρα αὐτοῦ,
καὶ παραμυθούμενοι αὐτὸν, σκέπουσιν τὸ πρόσωπον αὐτοῦ, ἵνα
μὴ ἴδῃ πῶς τιμωρεῖται αὐτὸς ὁ υἱὸς καὶ πλείονα φθαρῇ ἀπὸ τῆς
λύπης· οὕτως γάρ σε ἐλέησεν ὁ Θεὸς καὶ οὐκ ἔασέν σε ἐλθεῖν εἰς
Βαβυλῶνα· ἵνα μὴ ἴδῃς τὴν κάκωσιν τοῦ λαοῦ· ἀφ' ἧς γὰρ
εἰσήλθομεν εἰς τὴν πόλιν ταύτην, οὐκ ἐπαύσατο ἡ λύπη ἀφ'
ἡμῶν, ἑξήκοντα καὶ ἐξ ἔτη σήμερον. Πολλάκις γὰρ ἐξερχόμε- 25
νος ηὕρισκον ἐκ τοῦ λαοῦ κρεμαμένους ὑπὸ Ναβουχοδονόσορ
βασιλέως, κλαίοντας καὶ λέγοντας, Ἐλέησον ἡμᾶς, ὁ θεὸς Ζάρ.
Ἀκούων ταῦτα, ἐλυπούμην καὶ ἔκλαιον δισσὸν κλαυθμόν· οὐ 26
μόνον ὅτι ἐκρέμαντο, ἀλλ' ὅτι ἐπεκαλοῦντο θεὸν ἀλλότριον· λέγοντες, Ἐλέησον ἡμᾶς. Ἐμνημόνευον δὲ ἡμέρας ἑορτῆς ἃς ἐποιοῦ-
μεν ἐν Ἱερουσαλήμ· πρὸ τοῦ ἡμᾶς αἰχμαλωτευθῆναι. Καὶ μνησ- 27
κόμενος ἐστέναζον, καὶ ἐπέστρεφον εἰς τὸν οἶκόν μου ὀδυνώμενος
καὶ κλαίων. Νῦν οὖν δεήθητι, εἰς τὸν τόπον ὅπου εἶ, σὺ καὶ Ἀβιμέ- 28
λεχ, ὑπὲρ τοῦ λαοῦ τούτου, ὅπως εἰσακούσωσιν τῆς φωνῆς μου
καὶ τῶν κριμάτων τοῦ στόματός μου καὶ ἐξέλθωμεν ἐντεῦθεν.
Λέγω γάρ σοι, ὅτι ὅλον τὸν χρόνον ὃν ἐποιήσαμεν ἐνταῦθα, 29

v. 22 ημας; ab add Κυριος; not c aeth | for vv. 23...26; the text of ab is very
confused and varies a good deal from that which we have adopted from c aeth;
it runs as follows: εγραψε δε Ιερεμιας επιστολην εις Ιερουσαλημ προς Βαρουχ και
Ἀβιμελεχ ενωπιον παντος του λαου, τας θλιψεις τας (b om) γινομενας εις αυτους το
πως παρεληφθησαν υπο του βασιλεως των χαλδαιων· και το πως εκαστος τον πατερα
αυτου εθεωρει δεσμευομενον και πατηρ τεκνου παραδοθεν (b παραδοθεντα) εις τιμω-
ριαν· οι δε θελοντες παραμυθησασθαι τον πατερα αυτου σκεπουσι το προσωπον αυτου
ινα μη ιδη τον υιον αυτου τιμωρουμενον· και ο θεος εσκεπασεν σε και Ἀβιμελεχ· ινα
μη ιδηται ημας τιμωρουμενους | v. 23 κατευοδευση; c κατευοδοση | δικαιος γαρ ευρεθης; c
δικαιοι γαρ ευρεθησαν ; aeth du aber hast Gerechtigkeit vor Gott gefunden | μεθ' ημων
aeth; c om | v. 24 φθαρη; c φθαρει | οιτως; c ουτος | εις την πολιν ταυτην aeth;
εντανθα c | v. 25 κρεμαμενους; c κρεμμαμενους | Ζάρ (= Heb הר, αλλοτριος) ; c Σαβαωθ ;
miss aeth Zar, Sorot, Sarot | v. 27 οδυνωμενος (c) aeth; οδυρομενος ab | v. 28 νυν ουν
δεη. c aeth; ab δεηθητι ουν | εις τον τοπον οπου ει c aeth (wo ihr seid); ab om | εισα-
κουσωσιν...στοματος μου c aeth; ab εισακουσθη η δεησις υμων | κριματων; aeth ρηματων
(das Wort) | και εξ. εν. ab; c εξελθωσιν ενταυθα | v. 29 ολον; ab om (not c aeth).

κατέχουσιν ἡμᾶς λέγοντες ὅτι, Εἴπατε ἡμῖν ᾠδὴν ἐκ τῶν
ᾠδῶν Σιών, καὶ τὴν ᾠδὴν τοῦ Θεοῦ ὑμῶν. Καὶ ἀντελέγο-
30 μεν αὐτοῖς, Πῶς ᾄσωμεν ὑμῖν ἐπὶ γῆς ἀλλοτρίας ὄντες; Καὶ
μετὰ ταῦτα ἔδησε τὴν ἐπιστολὴν εἰς τὸν τράχηλον τοῦ ἀετοῦ,
λέγων, Ἄπελθε ἐν εἰρήνῃ, ἐπισκέψηται Κύριος ἀμφοτέρους.
31 Καὶ ἐπετάσθη ὁ ἀετὸς, καὶ ἤνεγκεν τὴν ἐπιστολὴν καὶ ἔδωκε
τῷ Βαρούχ. Καὶ λύσας ἀνέγνω, καὶ κατεφίλησεν αὐτὴν,
καὶ ἔκλαυσε ἀκούσας διὰ τὰς λύπας καὶ τὰς κακώσεις τοῦ
32 λαοῦ. Ἱερεμίας δὲ ἄρας τὰ σῦκα, διέδωκε τοῖς νοσοῦσι τοῦ
λαοῦ. Καὶ ἔμεινε διδάσκων αὐτοὺς τοῦ ἀπέχεσθαι ἐκ τῶν
ἀλισγημάτων τῶν ἐθνῶν τῆς Βαβυλῶνος.
1 VIII. Ἐγένετο δὲ ἡ ἡμέρα, ἐν ᾗ ἐξέφερε ὁ Θεὸς τὸν λαὸν
2 ἐκ Βαβυλῶνος· καὶ εἶπεν ὁ Κύριος πρὸς Ἱερεμίαν· Ἀνάστηθι,
σὺ καὶ ὁ λαὸς, καὶ δεῦτε ἐπὶ τὸν Ἰορδάνην, καὶ ἐρεῖς τῷ λαῷ,
Ὁ θέλων τὸν Κύριον καταλειψάτω τὰ ἔργα τῆς Βαβυλῶνος,
καὶ τοὺς ἄρρενας τοὺς λαβόντας ἐξ αὐτῶν γυναῖκας, καὶ τὰς
3 γυναῖκας τὰς λαβούσας ἐξ αὐτῶν ἄνδρας. Καὶ διαπεράσωσιν
οἱ ἀκούοντές σου, καὶ ἄρον αὐτοὺς εἰς Ἱερουσαλήμ· τοὺς δὲ μὴ
4 ἀκούοντάς σου, μὴ εἰσαγάγῃς αὐτοὺς εἰς αὐτήν. Ἱερεμίας δὲ ἐλάλησεν αὐτοῖς τὰ ῥήματα ταῦτα· καὶ ἀναστάντες ἦλθον ἐπὶ τὸν
Ἰορδάνην τοῦ περᾶσαι, λέγων αὐτοῖς τὰ ῥήματα, ἃ εἶπε Κύριος
πρὸς αὐτόν. Καὶ τὸ ἥμισυ τῶν γαμησάντων ἐξ αὐτῶν οὐκ ἠθέ-

v. 29 κατ. ημ. c aeth; ab ελεγον | και την; aeth καινην (sagt uns einen neuen
Gesang) | υμων; b ημων | αντελεγομεν ab; λεγωμεν c (? aeth) | ὑμῖν c aeth; ab την ᾠδην
κυριου | v. 30 αετου; ab add Ιερεμιας | κυριος αμφοτερους ab; c υμας αμφοτ. ο κ̅ς̅ | v. 31
επετασθη ab aeth; c om | αετος; ab add και ηλθεν εις (b om) Ιερουσαλημ | και ην...
Βαρουχ c, adding ο αετος after ηνεγκεν; ab και εδωκε την επιστολην Βαρουχ; aeth και
ηνεγκε την επιστολην τω Βαρουχ | εκλαυσε ab aeth; c εμεινε κλαιων | του λαου ab aeth;
c αυτων | v. 32 διεδωκε ab; εδωκε c (? aeth) | διδασκων; c ενδιδασκων (sic) | αλισγηματων
ab (α αλγηματων); c πραγματων; aeth das Thun und Treiben.
VIII. 1 ο θεος c aeth; ab κυριος | λαον; ab add αυτου (not c aeth) | προς Ιερεμιαν
ab; τω Ιερεμια c | end of verse ab add λεγων | v. 2 επι τον; a προς τον | τα εργα;
c aeth add των εθνων (from vii. 32) | λαβοντας ab; c (aeth) γαμησαντας | λαβουσας ab;
c (? aeth) γαμησαντας (sic) | v. 3 διαπερασωσιν ab; περασωσιν c | σου; b σοι | τους δε
μη ακουοντας ab; οι δε μη ακουοντες c | εισαγαγης ab; ενεγκης c | εις αυτην c aeth; εκει
ab | v. 4 αυτοις c aeth; ab προς τον λαον | αναστάντες ηλθον ab; ηνεγκεν αυτους c;
aeth (?) | κυριος προς αυτον; c αυτω ο Κυριος | και το ημισυ; at this point the text of c
abruptly drops from its level of excellence, and the manuscript ends with trivial
matter chiefly taken from the Septuagint; perhaps his copy was imperfect after the
word γαμησαντων; at all events his text proceeds as follows: και το ημισυ των γαμησαντων εξ αυτων αρω και στησω αυτοις διαθηκην αιωνιον του ειναι με αυτοις εις θεον· και
αυτοι εσονται μοι εις λαον· και ου κινησω τον λαον μου Ισραηλ απο της γης ης εδωκα
αυτοις· Κυριε, παντοκρατωρ, ὁ θεος Ισραηλ· ψυχη εν στενοις και πνευμα ακηδιον εκε-

λησαν ἀκοῦσαι τοῦ Ἰερεμίου, ἀλλ᾽ εἶπον πρὸς αὐτόν· Οὐ μὴ
καταλείψωμεν τὰς γυναῖκας ἡμῶν εἰς τὸν αἰῶνα· ἀλλ᾽ ὑποστρέ-
φωμεν αὐτὰς μεθ᾽ ἡμῶν εἰς τὴν πόλιν ἡμῶν. Ἐπέρασαν οὖν 5
τὸν Ἰορδάνην, καὶ ἦλθον εἰς Ἱερουσαλήμ. Καὶ ἔστη Ἰερεμίας,
καὶ Βαροὺχ καὶ Ἀβιμέλεχ, λέγοντες ὅτι, Πᾶς ἄνθρωπος κοι-
νῶν Βαβυλωνίταις οὐ μὴ εἰσέλθη εἰς τὴν πόλιν ταύτην. Καὶ 6
εἶπον πρὸς αὐτούς· Ἀναστάντες ὑποστρέψωμεν εἰς Βαβυλῶνα
εἰς τὸν τόπον ἡμῶν. Καὶ ἐπορεύθησαν. Ἐλθόντων δὲ αὐτῶν 7
εἰς Βαβυλῶνα, ἐξῆλθον οἱ Βαβυλωνῖται εἰς συνάντησιν αὐτῶν,
λέγοντες· Οὐ μὴ εἰσέλθητε εἰς τὴν πόλιν ἡμῶν, ὅτι ἐμισήσατε
ἡμᾶς, καὶ κρυφῇ ἐξήλθετε ἀφ᾽ ἡμῶν· διὰ τοῦτο οὐκ εἰσελεύ-

κραγεν προς σε· ακουσον, κυριε, και ελεησον· οτι θεος ελεων· και ελεησον οτι αμαρτανωμεν
εναντιον σου· οτι σοι καθημενος τον αιωνα ημεις απολλυμενοι τον αιωνα· κυριε, παντοκρατωρ,
ο θεος Ισραηλ, ακουσον δη της προσευχης των τεθνηκοτων Ισραηλ και υιων των αμαρτα-
νοντων εναντιον σου· οι ουκ ηκουσαν της φωνης θεου αυτων και εκολληθησαν ημιν τα
κακα· μη μνησθης (cod μνησθεις) αδικιων πατερων ημων· αλλα μνησθητι χειρος σου και
ονοματος σου εν τω καιρω τουτω· εγενετο δε μετα την συμπληρωσιν των εβδομηκοντα
ετων μεχρι του βασιλευσαι Περσας εν τω πρωτω ετει (cod ετη) Κυρου βασιλεως Περσων·
του τελεσθηναι λογον Κυριου απο στοματος Ιερεμιου εξηγειρεν κυριος το πνευμα Κυρου
βασιλεως Περσων· και παρηγγειλεν φωνην εν παση τη βασιλεια αυτου και αμα δια-
γραπτων λεγει· Ταδε λεγει Κυρος (cod Κ.) ο βασιλευς Περσων· πασας τας βασιλειας
της γης (cod om) εδωκεν μοι κυριος ο θεος του ουρανου· και αυτος επεσκεψατο επ᾽ εμε·
του οικοδομησαι αυτω (cod αυτον) οικον· εν Ιερουσαλημ τη εν τη Ιουδαια· ητις ουν
εστιν εκ του εθνους αυτου εστω ο Κυριος αυτου μετα αυτου· και αναβας εις την Ιερου-
σαλην την (cod τηνι) εν τη Ιουδαια οικοδομειτω (cod οκοδομιτω) τον οικον του θεου
Ισραηλ· ουτος (cod ουτως) ο Κυριος ο κατασκηνωσας εν Ιερουσαλημ· και ο βασιλευς
Κυρος εξηνεγκεν τα αγια σκευη (cod σκευει) του Κυριου· α μετηγαγεν Ναβουχοδονοσωρ
εξ Ιερουσαλημ. και...(cod απερησατω) αυτα εν τω ειδωλιω αυτου· εξηνεγκεν τα παντα
Κυρος ο βασιλευς Περσων και παρεδωκεν αυτα Μιθριδατη (cod Μηθρηδατη) τω εαυτου
γαζοφυλακι (cod γαζοφυλακη)· δια τουτου δε παρεδοθησαν Σαραβαρω προστατη της
Ιουδαιας· αμα Ζοροβαβελ ος (cod ως) και ητησατο επι Δαριου βασιλεως Περσων την
οικοδομην του ναου. ην γαρ κωλυσας επι τον Αρταξερξου χρονον ως ιστορησε Εσδρας·
τω δευτερω ετει (cod ετη) παραγενομενος εις το ιερον του θεου εις Ιερουσαλημ μηνος
δευτερου ηρξατο Ζοροβαβελ ο του Ραθαλαηλ και Ιησους ο του Ιωσεδεκα και οι αδελφοι
αυτων και οι ιερεις και οι Λευιται και παντες οι παραγενομενοι εκ της αιχμαλωσιας
εις Ιερουσαλημ· και εθεμελιωσαν τον οικον του θεου τη νουμηνια του δευτερου μηνος·
εν τω ελθειν εις την Ιουδαιαν και Ιερουσαλημ· προφητευοντων Αγγεου και Ζαχαριου
υιου Αδδων· τελευταιων (cod τελευτεων) προφητων· ανεβη δε ο Εσδρας εκ Βαβυλωνος
ως γραμματευς ευφυης ων εν τω Μωυσεως νομω· ος (cod ως) και επιστημην πολλην
ειχεν τω διδασκειν αυτον (cod αυτω) απαντα τον λαον τα δικαιωματα και τα κριματα
επι τον Αρταξερξου χρονον· και εποιησαν εγκαινια του οικου του θεου, υμνουντες και
ευλογουντες τω κυριω επι τη εγερσει του οικου του θεου.
v. 4 εις την πολιν ημων aeth; ab εις Βαβυλωνα | v. 5 κοινων; b κοινωνων | ταυτην;
aeth ημων | v. 6 και ειπον; aeth adds οι γαμησαντες γυναικας (welche eine Weib
geheiratet hätten) | εις τον τοπον ημων; aeth om | επορευθησαν; aeth adds και υπε-
στρεψαν | v. 7 ου μη...ημων; aeth om | εμισησατε; aeth adds vorher.

σεσθε πρὸς ἡμᾶς. Ὅρκῳ γὰρ ὠρκίσαμεν ἀλλήλους κατὰ τοῦ ὀνόματος τοῦ θεοῦ ἡμῶν, μήτε ὑμᾶς μήτε τέκνα ὑμῶν δέξασθαι,
8 ἐπειδὴ κρυφῇ ἐξήλθετε ἀφ᾽ ἡμῶν. Καὶ ἐπιγνόντες ὑπέστρεψαν· καὶ ἦλθον εἰς τόπον ἔρημον μακρόθεν τῆς Ἱερουσαλὴμ, καὶ ᾠκοδόμησαν ἑαυτοῖς πόλιν, καὶ ἐπωνόμασαν τὸ ὄνομα αὐτῆς
9 Σαμάρειαν. Ἀπέστειλε δὲ πρὸς αὐτοὺς Ἱερεμίας, λέγων· Μετανοήσατε· ἔρχεται γὰρ ἄγγελος τῆς δικαιοσύνης, καὶ εἰσάξει ὑμᾶς εἰς τὸν τόπον ὑμῶν τὸν ὑψηλόν.
1 IX. Ἔμειναν δὲ οἱ τοῦ Ἱερεμίου, χαίροντες καὶ ἀναφέροντες
2 θυσίαν ὑπὲρ τοῦ λαοῦ ἐννέα ἡμέρας. Τῇ δὲ δεκάτῃ ἀνήνεγκεν
3 Ἱερεμίας μόνος θυσίαν, καὶ ηὔξατο εὐχὴν, λέγων· Ἅγιος, ἅγιος, ἅγιος· τὸ θυμίαμα τῶν δένδρων τῶν ζώντων, τὸ φῶς τὸ ἀληθινὸν Joh. i. 9. τὸ φωτίζον με, ἕως οὗ ἀναληφθῶ πρὸς σὲ, περὶ τῆς φωνῆς τῆς
4 γλυκείας τῶν δύο Σεραφίμ. Παρακαλῶ ὑπὲρ ἄλλης εὐωδίας
5 θυμιάματος· καὶ ἡ μελέτη μου Μιχαὴλ ὁ ἀρχάγγελος τῆς
6 δικαιοσύνης, ἕως ἂν εἰσενέγκῃ τοὺς δικαίους. Παρακαλῶ σε, Κύριε παντοκράτωρ πάσης κτίσεως, ὁ ἀγέννητος καὶ ἀπερινόητος, ᾧ πᾶσα κρίσις κέκρυπται ἐν αὐτῷ πρὸ τοῦ ταῦτα
7 γενέσθαι. Ταῦτα λέγοντος τοῦ Ἱερεμίου, καὶ ἱσταμένου ἐν τῷ θυσιαστηρίῳ μετὰ Βαροὺχ καὶ Ἀβιμέλεχ, ἐγένετο ὡς εἷς
8 τῶν παραδιδόντων τὴν ψυχὴν αὐτοῦ. Καὶ ἔμειναν Βαροὺχ καὶ Ἀβιμέλεχ κλαίοντες, καὶ κράζοντες μεγάλῃ τῇ φωνῇ ὅτι, Ὁ πατὴρ ἡμῶν Ἱερεμίας κατέλιπεν ἡμᾶς, ὁ ἱερεὺς τοῦ Θεοῦ,
9 καὶ ἀπῆλθεν. Ἤκουσε δὲ πᾶς ὁ λαὸς τοῦ κλαυθμοῦ αὐτῶν, καὶ ἔδραμον ἐπ᾽ αὐτοὺς πάντες, καὶ εἶδον Ἱερεμίαν ἀνακείμενον χαμαὶ τεθνηκότα· καὶ διέρρηξαν τὰ ἱμάτια αὐτῶν, καὶ ἐπέθηκαν χοῦν ἐπὶ τὰς κεφαλὰς αὐτῶν, καὶ ἔκλαυσαν κλαυθμὸν πικρόν.
10 Καὶ μετὰ ταῦτα ἡτοίμασαν ἑαυτοὺς, ἵνα κηδεύσωσιν αὐτόν.

v. 7 προς ημας; aeth εις την πολιν ημων.

IX. 1 οι του Ιερεμιου; aeth om | εννεα; aeth επτα | v. 3 το θυμιαμα...ζωντων; aeth angenehmer Wohlgeruch den Menschen | προς σε; aeth ich flehe dich an wegen deines Volkes und ich bitte dich | v. 4 παρακαλω υπερ (b περι)...θυμιαματος; aeth und um des Weihrauchduftes der Cherubim (και περι ευωδιας θυμιαματος των χερουβιμ) | v. 5 aeth ich bitte dich dass doch ja der gesangskundige Michael, der Engel der Gerechtigkeit ist er, die Pforten der Gerechtigkeit offen halte, bis sie in dieselben einziehen | v. 6 Κυριε; b om | κυριε...γενεσθαι; aeth Herr über alles und Herr welcher alles umfasst und alles erschaffen hat, welcher erscheint und welcher nicht geboren ist, welcher alles vollendet hat und bei dem die ganze Schöpfung verborgen war, ehe die Dinge im Verborgenen gemacht wurden | v. 7 ταυτα...Ιερεμιου; aeth und dies betete er und als er sein Gebet geendet hatte | v. 8 και εμειναν; aeth und alsbald fielen B. und A. nieder.

Καὶ ἰδοὺ φωνὴ ἦλθε, λέγουσα· Μὴ κηδεύετε τὸν ἔτι ζῶντα· 11
ὅτι ἡ ψυχὴ αὐτοῦ εἰσέρχεται εἰς τὸ σῶμα αὐτοῦ πάλιν. Καὶ 12
ἀκούσαντες τῆς φωνῆς, οὐκ ἐκήδευσαν αὐτὸν, ἀλλ᾽ ἔμειναν
περικύκλῳ τοῦ σκηνώματος αὐτοῦ ἡμέρας τρεῖς, λέγοντες καὶ
ἀποροῦντες, ποίᾳ ὥρᾳ μέλλει ἀναστῆναι. Μετὰ δὲ τρεῖς ἡμέρας 13
εἰσῆλθεν ἡ ψυχὴ αὐτοῦ εἰς τὸ σῶμα αὐτοῦ· καὶ ἐπῆρε τὴν
φωνὴν αὐτοῦ ἐν μέσῳ πάντων, καὶ εἶπε· Δοξάσατε τὸν Θεὸν,
πάντες δοξάσατε τὸν Θεὸν, καὶ τὸν Υἱὸν τοῦ Θεοῦ τὸν ἐξυπνί-
ζοντα ἡμᾶς Ἰησοῦν Χριστὸν, τὸ φῶς τῶν αἰώνων πάντων, ὁ
ἄσβεστος λύχνος, ἡ ζωὴ τῆς πίστεως. Γίνεται δὲ μετὰ τοὺς 14
καιροὺς τούτους ἄλλα ἔτη τετρακόσια ἑβδομηκονταεπτὰ, καὶ
ἔρχεται εἰς τὴν γῆν· καὶ τὸ δένδρον τῆς ζωῆς τὸ ἐν μέσῳ τοῦ
παραδείσου φυτευθὲν ποιήσει πάντα τὰ δένδρα τὰ ἄκαρπα

Cf. Ign.
ad Trall.
XI. 2.

ποιῆσαι καρπὸν, καὶ αὐξηθήσονται, καὶ βλαστήσουσι, *καὶ
ὁ καρπὸς αὐτῶν μετὰ τῶν ἀγγέλων μενεῖ.* Καὶ τὰ βεβλα- 15
στηκότα, καὶ μεγαλαυχοῦντα, καὶ λέγοντα, Ἐδώκαμεν τὸ
τέλος ἡμῶν τῷ ἀέρι· ποιήσει αὐτὰ ξηρανθῆναι μετὰ τοῦ ὕψους
τῶν κλάδων αὐτῶν· καὶ ποιήσει αὐτὰ κλιθῆναι* τὸ δένδρον
τὸ στηριχθέν· καὶ ποιήσει τὸ κόκκινον ὡς ἔριον λευκὸν γενέσθαι.
Ἡ χιὼν μελανθήσεται, τὰ γλυκέα ὕδατα ἁλμυρὰ γενήσονται 16
ἐν τῷ μεγάλῳ φωτὶ τῆς εὐφροσύνης τοῦ Θεοῦ. Καὶ εὐλογήσει 17
τὰς νήσους τοῦ ποιῆσαι καρπὸν ἐν τῷ λόγῳ τοῦ στόματος τοῦ
Χριστοῦ αὐτοῦ. Αὐτὸς γὰρ ἐλεύσεται, καὶ ἐξελεύσεται, καὶ 18
ἐπιλέξεται ἑαυτῷ δώδεκα ἀποστόλους, ἵνα εὐαγγελίζωνται ἐν
τοῖς ἔθνεσιν· ὃν ἐγὼ ἑώρακα κεκοσμημένον ὑπὸ τοῦ Πατρὸς
αὐτοῦ, καὶ ἐρχόμενον εἰς τὸν κόσμον ἐπὶ τὸ ὄρος τῶν ἐλαιῶν·
καὶ ἐμπλήσει τὰς πεινώσας ψυχάς. Ταῦτα λέγοντος τοῦ 19

v. 11 κηδευετε; b κηδευσατε; aeth wickelt ihn nicht in Leinen; so in v. 12 |
v. 12 εμειναν...αναστηναι; aeth sassen indem sie um ihn drei Tage wachten bis
seine Seele in seinen Körper zurückkehrte | v. 13 μετα...φωνην αυτου; aeth und eine
Stimme erscholl | τον θεον (2ˢ); aeth τον χριστον (den Gesalbten) | εξυπνιζοντα;
aeth auferwecken und richten | v. 14 ετη τετρ. εβδ. ab; aeth 303 (codd. 330, 333)
Wochen von Tagen | και το δενδρον aeth; των δενδρων ab | φυτευθεν; aeth war
und nicht gepflanzt war | και...μενει; ab om; aeth und ihre Frucht wird bei
den Engeln wohnen | v. 15 βεβλαστηκοτα; a βεβληκοτα | μετα...κλιθηναι (b κρι-
θηναι); a om | the whole verse thus in aeth; und um der Pflanzschule der Bäume
willen, damit sie grün werden und hoch wachsen, wollen wie der Luft Verherrlichung
spenden damit ihre Wurzeln nicht ausdürren wie eine Pflanze deren Wurzel nicht
Boden gefasst hat | και ποιησει aeth; και ab | ως aeth; και ab | v. 16 τα γλυκεα...γενη-
σονται; aeth adds και τα αλμυρα γλυκεα γενησονται | εν...θεου; aeth mit grossem
Frohlocken und die Freuden Gottes | v. 17 χριστου; aeth μου | v. 18 ινα ευαγ. ...
εωρακα; aeth damit ihnen gezeigt werde was ich gesehen habe | κεκοσμημενον ab;
aeth geschickt | πεινωσας a aeth; ταπεινωσας b.

Ἰερεμίου περὶ τοῦ Υἱοῦ τοῦ Θεοῦ, ὅτι ἔρχεται εἰς τὸν κόσμον,
20 ὠργίσθη ὁ λαὸς, καὶ εἶπε· Ταῦτα πάλιν ἐστὶ τὰ ῥήματα τὰ
ὑπὸ Ἡσαΐου τοῦ υἱοῦ Ἀμὼς εἰρημένα, λέγοντος ὅτι, Εἶδον
21 τὸν Θεὸν, καὶ τὸν Υἱὸν τοῦ Θεοῦ. Δεῦτε οὖν, καὶ μὴ ἀποκτεί-
νωμεν αὐτὸν τῷ ἐκείνου θανάτῳ, ἀλλὰ λίθοις λιθοβολήσωμεν
22 αὐτόν. Ἐλυπήθησαν σφόδρα ἐπὶ τῇ ἀπονοίᾳ ταύτῃ Βαροὺχ
καὶ Ἀβιμέλεχ, καὶ ὅτι ἤθελον ἀκοῦσαι πλήρης τὰ μυστήρια,
23 ἃ εἶδε. Λέγει δὲ αὐτοῖς Ἰερεμίας· Σιωπήσατε, καὶ μὴ κλαίετε·
24 οὐ μὴ γάρ με ἀποκτείνωσιν, ἕως οὗ πάντα ὅσα εἶδον διηγή-
25 σωμαι ὑμῖν. Εἶπε δὲ αὐτοῖς· Ἐνέγκατέ μοι λίθον. Ὁ δὲ ἔστησεν
αὐτὸν, καὶ εἶπε· Τὸ φῶς τῶν αἰώνων, ποίησον τὸν λίθον τοῦτον
26 καθ᾽ ὁμοιότητά μου γενέσθαι. Ὁ δὲ λίθος ἀνέλαβεν ὁμοιότητα
27 τοῦ Ἰερεμίου. Καὶ ἐλιθοβόλουν τὸν λίθον, νομίζοντες ὅτι
28 Ἰερεμίας ἐστίν. Ὁ δὲ Ἰερεμίας πάντα παρέδωκε τὰ μυστήρια,
29 ἃ εἶδε, τῷ Βαροὺχ καὶ τῷ Ἀβιμέλεχ. Καὶ εἶθ᾽ οὕτως ἔστη
ἐν μέσῳ τοῦ λαοῦ, ἐκτελέσαι βουλόμενος τὴν οἰκονομίαν αὐτοῦ.
30 Ἐβόησε δὲ ὁ λίθος, λέγων· Ὦ μωροὶ υἱοὶ Ἰσραὴλ, διὰ τί
λιθοβολεῖτέ με, νομίζοντες ὅτι ἐγὼ Ἰερεμίας; Ἰδοὺ Ἰερεμίας
31 ἐν μέσῳ ὑμῶν ἵσταται. Ὡς δὲ εἶδον αὐτὸν, εὐθέως ἔδραμον
πρὸς αὐτὸν μετὰ πολλῶν λίθων. Καὶ ἐπληρώθη αὐτοῦ οἰκο-
32 νομία. Καὶ ἐλθόντες Βαροὺχ καὶ Ἀβιμέλεχ, ἔθαψαν αὐτὸν,
καὶ λαβόντες τὸν λίθον ἔθηκαν ἐπὶ τὸ μνῆμα αὐτοῦ, ἐπιγρά-
ψαντες οὕτως· Οὗτός ἐστιν ὁ λίθος ὁ βοηθὸς τοῦ Ἰερεμίου.

v. 20 και; aeth om | v. 21 μη αποκτεινωμεν κτέ; aeth wir wollen an ihm
handeln wie wir an Jesaias gehandelt haben; und ein Theil von ihnen sagte, Nein,
fürwahr, mit Steinen werden wir ihn werfen. Und Baruch und Abemelek schrieen
ihnen zu, Durch diese Todesart tödtet ihn nicht | v. 22 πληρης b; πληρη a |
v. 24 end; aeth adds και ηνεγκαν αυτω λιθον | v. 25 εστησεν; b ανεστησεν | μου;
aeth avov | γενεσθαι; ab adds εως ου παντα οσα ιδον διηγησωμαι τω Βαρουχ και τω
Αβιμελεχ | v. 26 λιθος; ab add δια προσταγματος θεου | v. 29 ειθ᾽ ουτως; b ειθ᾽ αυτως
(sic) | v. 30 εν μεσω; b εις μεσον | v. 32 ο λιθος; aeth om | end of verse ab add και τα
λοιπα των λογων Ιερεμιου και πασα η δυναμις· ουκ ιδου (a om) ενταυθα εγγεγραπται εν
τη επιστολη Βαρουχ.

www.ingramcontent.com/pod-product-compliance
Lightning Source LLC
Chambersburg PA
CBHW032043090426
42733CB00030B/644